PLANT TRAINING, PRUNING AND TREE SURGERY

ABOUT THIS BOOK

This book is about plant shape and how it may be modified to suit man's needs. Today, as never before, we live in such close proximity to one another that crop plants have to produce maximum yields in the areas available to them, and ornamental plants are often required to fit into limited and difficult sites.

Plant Training, Pruning and Tree Surgery looks at these problems, discussing why plants need to be trained, what determines plant shape, and what methods are available to modify it.

Throughout, the emphasis is placed on basic principles—*why* things happen, rather than just *how-to*. Early chapters are devoted to basic information on plant structure and function and form a background to later chapters where specific plant subjects are discussed in detail.

Plants are considered in relation to both their normal life form and the use to which they are put. Particular emphasis is placed on the importance of aesthetic considerations when dealing with such visually important subjects as trees.

Ample illustrations are included in the form of colour plates, monochrome photographs and line drawings. These are particularly important in a book of this type and, taken with the text, will enable the home gardener to train successfully any of the plants dealt with in the book.

WIND-PRUNED MANUKA *(Leptospermum scoparium)*
Buds on the windward side of the tree become dehydrated and damaged to a greater extent than those on the leeward side. This leads to uneven growth in relation to the prevailing wind. This is a dramatic example of the influence of the environment on plant shape.

FELL'S GUIDE TO
Plant Training, Pruning and Tree Surgery

K. R. W. HAMMETT

BSc(Hons), PhD

Line drawings by Christine M. Hammett and the author
Photographs by Alan Underhill and the author

A World of Books That Fill a Need

FREDERICK FELL PUBLISHERS, Inc.   NEW YORK

Manufactured and printed in Japan
First published in New Zealand by:
A.H. & A.W. Reed Ltd
182 Wakefield Street, Wellington

For information address:
Frederick Fell Publishers, Inc.
386 Park Avenue South
New York, N.Y. 10016

In Canada:
George J. McLeod Limited
Toronto 2B, Ontario

International Standard Book Number 0-8119-0260-9

Library of Congress Catalog Card No. 75-583

Typeset on IBM Composer by A.H. & A.W. Reed Ltd, Wellington
Printed and bound by Kyodo-Shing Loong Printing Industries Pte Ltd., Singapore

CONTENTS

PREFACE   9

INTRODUCTION   10

PART I
Chapter 1   *What Is a Plant?*
             Structure; roots; aerial parts; life cycle of annuals, biennials,
             herbaceous perennials and woody perennials.   13
Chapter 2   *Growth*
             Apical dominance.   16
Chapter 3   *Stem Structure and Function*
Chapter 4   *Ways to Train Plants*
             Mechanical; budding and grafting; plant tropisms; plant breeding;
             chemical plant control—auxins, gibberellins, cytokinins, abscisins,
             ethylene generators, growth retardants (Maleic hydrazide,
             Chlormequat, Alar -85).   21

PART II
Chapter 5   *The One-Year Framework*
             Tomatoes; cucumbers; sweet peas; dahlias; chrysanthemums.   29
Chapter 6   *Woody Perennial Plants*
             A. *Ornamentals*—Fuchsia training (basic shapes; bush; standard;
             fan, espalier, pillar and pyramid); topiary; formal hedges.
             B. *Dwarf or Bonsai Trees.*
             C. *Fruit and Roses*—SOFT FRUIT (blackberries, boysenberries
             and loganberries; raspberries; black currants; red and white
             currants; gooseberries). TREE FRUIT—Pip fruit (apples—i. Training
             a new tree. ii. The old-established tree; pears). Stone fruit (apricots;
             peaches and nectarines; cherries; plums). CITRUS—Subtropicals
             (feijoas; tree tomatoes; passion fruit; chinese gooseberries). GRAPE
             VINES. ROSES (hybrid tea roses; floribunda roses; rambler roses;
             climbing roses; shrub roses, miniature roses).   35

PART III
Chapter 7   *Tree Surgery*
             Damaged and diseased parts; limb removal; cavity treatment;
             bracing and cabling. *Aesthetic considerations*—ways to prune
             trees (pollarding; heading, etc; thinning and lifting).
             Time of year to prune and knowledge of species.   52

APPENDIX I
             Budding and grafting.   62

APPENDIX II
             Tools and pruning cuts.   65

APPENDIX III
             Book list for further reading.   66

INDEX   67

PHOTOGRAPHS

PLATE

Frontispiece. Wind-pruned manuka.

1	*Pinus radiata* grown in open	11
2	*Pinus radiata* grown closely planted	11
3	Grazing sheep as an environmental factor	11
4	Plants grown in lines for weed control	11
5	Rosette plants	14
6 & 7	Dormant and adventitious buds growing from a stump	18
8	Plant showing negative geotropism	22
9	Plant showing positive geotropism	22
10	Tomato plants trained as single cordons	29
11	Hothouse cucumbers trained to make the best use of light	30
12	Shrub that has lost its "natural" shape through trimming	35
13	Topped Norfolk Island pine (main growing point removed)	35
14	Mutilated pohutukawa showing atypical growth	36
15	Trees too large for the garden	36
16	Man's dominance over the landscape (18th century illustration)	36

PLATE

17	Dead branch removal (first stage in pruning)	53
18	Fencing wire embedded in the stem of a tree	53
19	Slow overgrowth of a wound on a tree	54
20	Wound left when a limb is correctly removed	54
21	Stubs should never be left on a tree	56
22	Removal of tree limbs in sections	56
23	Wound dressing after tree surgery	57
24	Pollarded street tree	59
25	Thinning and slight lifting of tree	60
26	Thinned tree	61

APPENDIX I

27	Bud removed by single knife cut	63
28	Inserting the bud	63
29	Binding-in the bud	63
30	Removing the head of the stock plant	63
31	Dressing the resultant wound	64
32	The scion bud growing	64
33	Head formed on the stock roots	64

COLOUR PLATES

COLOUR PLATES

1 - 4	Stages in the development of a pyramid Fuchsia	25
5 - 7	Stages in the development of a standard Fuchsia	26
8 - 9	Stages in the development of a bush Fuchsia	26
10 - 14	Various stages in the production of sweet pea blooms by the cordon system	27 - 28
15	Rose understock *Rosa multiflora* clone IOWA 60/5	28
16	*Rosa chinensis* 'Major' sometimes used as an understock	28

LIST OF FIGURES

FIGURE

1	Balance between aerial and root growth	13
2	Shoot morphology	16
3	Bud orientation	16
4	Longitudinal section of a bud	16
5	Apical dominance	17
6	Transverse section through stems	19
7	Movement within woody stems	20
8	Tomato grown on the cordon system	29
9	Stopping and formation of basal shoots in sweet pea	31
10	Wings and stipules become expanded in response to the cordon system of sweet pea training	31
11	Use of plant tropism in cordon training of sweet pea	32
12	Dahlia training	33
13	Chrysanthemum training	33
14	Chrysanthemum disbudding	34
15	Bush Fuchsia	37
16	Standard Fuchsias	38
17	Poorly-constructed standard Fuchsia	38
18	Stages in the development of an espalier Fuchsia	38
19	Stages in the development of a fan Fuchsia	39
20	Pyramid and pillar Fuchsias	39
21	Fuchsias in hanging baskets	39
22	Various topiary shapes	39
23	Hedge shapes	40
24	Bonsai tree	41
25	Blackberry, Boysenberry and Loganberry	41

FIGURE

26	Raspberries	42
27	Blackcurrants	42
28	Red and white currants	42
29	Gooseberries	43
30	Spindle-shaped tree suitable for apples and pears	44
31	Crotch shape in tree	44
32	Vase-shaped tree	45
33	Standard tree	46
34	Passion fruit	48
35	Chinese gooseberry on single wire system	48
36	Grape vine	49
37	Open cup-shaped framework for hybrid tea rose	51
38	Tree limb removal (1)	55
39	Tree limg removal (2)	55
40	Cavity treatment in trees	57
41	Draining a tree cavity	57
42	A well-filled tree cavity	57
43	Cabling and bracing	58
44	Triangular cabling of tree	58
45	A headed tree	59
46	"Lifting"	61

APPENDIX I

47	Budding—main steps	62
48	Whip and tongue grafting	64

APPENDIX II

49	Correct and incorrect pruning cuts	65

BACK COVER PICTURES

A An apple tree being trained on the spindle system. Note how branches are being tied to a horizontal position with twine.

B A good crop of pears borne on the lowest branch of a spindle tree.

C Fruit of the Chinese gooseberry, variety 'Abbot'. One fruit cut in half to show structure.

D A well cared-for fruit tree can be an object of beauty in all seasons. This plum tree forms the focal point of this small garden.

DEDICATION

To Christine, Timothy and Christopher

K.R.W. HAMMETT was born at Epsom, England, in 1942 and was educated at Tiffin Boys' School, Kingston-upon-Thames, and Southampton University. He came to New Zealand in 1967 to work as a plant pathologist at the Plant Diseases Division of the Department of Scientific & Industrial Research. He lives in Auckland, is married and has two sons.

Horticulture has been Dr Hammett's main interest since he was a teenager. In England he was an exhibitor and judge at both local and national shows. He served on the committees of various societies, including the National Sweet Pea Society, and contributed numerous articles to horticultural publications.

With the popular *Plant Propagation* (1973), his first publication in the Reedway Garden Books series, Dr Hammett showed he is an expert with the rare ability to convey experience and knowledge in easily-assimilable terms.

He has also written regularly for the *New Zealand Gardener* and other publications in New Zealand and overseas, has lectured widely, and has served on the organising committees of the Garden Week Shows held in Auckland in 1968 and 1970, from which he has derived a keen interest in the New Zealand nursery industry

The hybridisation and genetics of sweet peas are his special interest, and a breeding programme being carried out by Dr Hammett is producing some interesting developments for the future.

8

PREFACE

THE SUBJECT of pruning has many books devoted to it, while training and tree surgery are most commonly treated as chapters in books on more general topics. This book attempts to treat the subject of plant shape as a whole. This is in keeping with other fields where traditional demarcations are, today, more of a barrier to understanding than a help.

This book explores three central themes: (1) What are the objectives of training plants? (2) What are the methods available for regulating plant growth? (3) What are the limitations of plant response?

Throughout, the emphasis is placed on basic principles, so that anyone reading the book will be able to gain an understanding of the factors involved in controlling plant shape. Early chapters are devoted to basic information on plant structure and function. This is intended as a background for the more practical information dealing with specific plants.

It is impossible in a book of this size to obtain comprehensive coverage and at the same time give equal weight to each plant. I have therefore tried to provide more information on those subjects poorly covered elsewhere and less for those where sound texts are readily available. I have, however, tried to cover in sufficient detail the main plants which require training so that home gardeners may obtain satisfactory results. In doing this I have selected what I consider to be the method best suited to the home garden. A book list is appended for those requiring details of alternative methods for any subject.

I have tried to draw attention to the use of rootstocks and their significance, as a great many home gardeners are unaware of this aspect of plant production.

Tree surgery is treated in detail, as this subject is rapidly increasing in importance as man becomes more concerned with his environment. Trees contribute significantly to both rural and urban landscapes, and if this book helps in only a small measure to reduce the mutilation of home and street trees, it will have been well justified.

K.R.W. Hammett

INTRODUCTION

AT THE OUTSET it is important to realise that plants do not need man. They have survived and evolved over countless millions of years, long before man came into being. Man, on the other hand, is dependent on plants in a great many ways—indeed his very existence depends upon them. Plants form the basis of all food chains and play a vital role in maintaining the level of oxygen in the atmosphere. In addition man exploits plants for a very large and varied range of products and derives aesthetic pleasures from the shape, colours and scents of plants.

Plants occur in many forms and sizes and some of the most important are the microscopic phytoplankton which live in the oceans of the world. Generally, however, man concerns himself mainly with the larger flowering plants which live on land and it is with these that we will deal in this book.

In cultivating a plant man inevitably has a profound influence on its shape. Sometimes this is deliberate, more often it is quite incidental. For instance, an individual tree grown as a specimen in a park assumes a different form to another individual of the same species grown in a forest. Grazing a field with sheep radically alters the shape of plants affected, besides eliminating those plants which cannot withstand such treatment. In these instances man alters the balance of ecological forces acting upon any one plant. These in turn affect its shape. In the first case the mutual competition of the forest trees is the ecological factor and in the second it is the sheep.

Very often man seeks deliberately to alter the shape of a plant so that a special feature of that plant is enhanced. The aim may be to obtain more fruit, or more leaves, or to improve the quality of fruit, or to make a plant more decorative. In such cases man is acting as a direct ecological factor. To act successfully in this role we must:

a) have a clear and precise idea of what we are trying to achieve
b) have a broad understanding of how a plant works
c) know the limitations of the plant under consideration and
d) know what methods are available to achieve these aims.

These are the ideas which will be explored and applied throughout this book.

PLATE 1
Pinus radiata
Grown in the open as a specimen tree. Light from all directions has produced a short trunk, a crown of several main branches and a wide spreading canopy.

PLATE 2
Pinus radiata
Grown closely planted to form a deep shelter belt. Competition between the trees for light has produced long straight trunks with realtively small side branches.

PLATE 3
Grazing sheep are a powerful environmental factor, which under Man's management have a profound effect on plant shape and the landscape. On one side of the fence the grass is long, while on the other side it forms a dense turf as a result of constant grazing.

PLATE 4
Man grows plants in lines so that he may control weeds by mechanical means. In doing this he eliminates all plants which would compete with his crop plants, thus altering the habitat and consequently the shape of his crop plant.

PART I

1

What Is a Plant?

EVEN THE SIMPLEST plant is a complex living organism and plant scientists are a long way from having a full understanding of just how a plant works. However, our understanding of plants is far greater than it was only a few years ago and it is important for anyone wishing to train plants to have a clear idea of their structure and some idea of the processes going on within them.

Structure

Land plants are remarkable organisms in that they inhabit two quite different environments; one above ground and the other below.

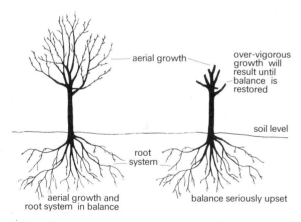

FIG 1. Balance between aerial and root growth.

It is difficult to imagine two more divergent environments, especially as they are so close spacially. These differences are clearly reflected in the different form of a plant's aerial parts and those below ground.

Roots

Soil is the medium in which most plant roots live and perform their functions. Soils vary widely in detail, but basically they are complex organisations of particles of various types and sizes. They possess water in which substances are dissolved, they contain air and vast numbers of different soil organisms. Such an environment exerts a considerable physical pressure on any plant organ living in it, and, being dense, any organ wishing to grow through such a medium must be flexible so that areas of weakness may be located and successfully negotiated. Both the morphology (external shape) and internal anatomy of roots fulfil these specifications. Roots are almost invariably cylindrical, the shape best suited to withstand external pressures, and their internal anatomy confers flexibility rather than rigidity.

The precise form of root systems and the depth of their penetration into the soil varies with different species and different soil types. The functions of roots are, however, common to all plants. These are the absorption of water and minerals from soils; the firm anchorage of the whole plant; the transport of substances both to and from the aerial parts; and the storage of many types of foodstuff.

In many plants the depth of the mature roots is often greater than the height of the stems above ground. Spectacular figures are produced from time to time to show the extent of root systems. For example, a single rye plant has been claimed to have a total of 13,815,762 roots with a combined length of 623 km (387 miles) and a total surface area of 237 km^2 (2,554 sq.ft), which would be about 130 times the surface area of all the aerial parts. Daily linear root growth of such a root system would be about 5 km (3 miles). Different plants produce different proportions of root to top growth, but the significance of such extensive root growth is that movement of water in soils towards roots is limited and roots have to grow into new regions of soil to obtain supplies.

This book will not concern itself any further with the root systems of plants, but it is important to remember that an untouched or undamaged plant establishes and maintains a balance between the aerial parts and its root system. Any interference with the aerial parts upsets this balance; this must be borne carefully in mind.

Aerial Parts

The area immediately above soil level has one of the most vicious environments imaginable, even in equable climates. Aerial parts of plants have to contend with large temperature fluctuations between day and night, intense radiation of various types, rain, hail, snow and winds, which may be of low moisture content and thus place considerable drying stress on plants besides straightforward mechanical stress. Humans and many animals quickly die in such an environment unless they are protected by shelter or clothing. Besides just existing under such conditions, the leaves of green plants have to carry out the vital process of photosynthesis.

Photosynthesis is the fundamental process of food manufacture in nature. Expressed in very simple terms, leaves use or capture the energy of the sun and combine carbon dioxide, from the air, with water from the soil to produce sugars. These are the basic food from which all other kinds of foods and other organic compounds in plants and animals are manufactured. Photosynthesis and the green plants in which it takes place are the basis of life on this planet. Needless to say, it is a complex process, still not fully understood.

Although it is several centuries now since man first started to realise the role of leaves, many people even today do not think of leaves as radiation-receiving organs and still tend to think that plants derive all their nourishment from minerals taken up from the soil.

Life Cycle

The vast diversity of plant shape represents many slightly different solutions to the problem of coping with the difficult environmental stresses and at the same time presenting the leaves in the most effective way to make use of the sun's energy. Such considerations are most important when we come to train a plant.

Gardeners loosely classify plants on the basis of a combination of plant shape and the length of time they live and support aerial growth. The main groupings are as follows:

ANNUALS

Plants which develop from seed, flower, fruit and die within one year.

BIENNIALS

Plants which occupy two growing seasons to complete their life cycle. The plant is formed in the first season and then flowers, fruits and dies in the second.

HERBACEOUS PERENNIALS

Plants which exist for a number of growing seasons (perennial) and die down to or near ground level annually.

WOODY PERENNIALS

Plants which exist for a number of growing seasons and have an aerial framework which is added to each growing season.

Annual and biennial plants are raised from seed and as they have a relatively short life span they are less subject to training than many perennial plants. Notable exceptions to this generalisation are the sweet pea, an annual plant whose training to produce exhibition standard flowers has reached a high degree of skill, and crop plants such as cucumbers and tomatoes. Annual plants develop a framework of stems and shoots on which the leaves and flowers are borne. The shape of this framework is determined

PLATE 5
Many plants form low rosetted growth for much of the year, producing appreciable stems only at flowering time. This is one solution that plants have made in coping with environmental stresses.

by the genetic characteristics of the particular plant. This is seldom modified other than to pinch the growing point out of some plants at the time of planting. This has the effect of making the plants more bushy and compact.

Biennials frequently form rosette-shaped plants in their first season. Here the leaves are borne on a very short stem and thus appear to form a rosette. It is only in the second season that an appreciable stem is formed on which the flowers are borne.

Many herbaceous perennials behave in the same way and form mats of tufted growth each year from which a flowering framework is formed in the following season. As with annuals relatively little training is carried out on plants of this type other than to cut away the dead flowering framework and to perhaps thin the shoots in the spring. Again a notable exception is the chrysanthemum which is subject to special training for specific purposes.

An important group of herbaceous perennial plants are those which have bulbs, corms or tubers and die right down to below the ground each year. These are seldom trained, but yet again an exception is the Dahlia when used as a cut flower or exhibition plant.

Woody perennials are the plants most commonly thought of as subjects worthy of training. An important distinction is made between shrubs, which form a number of persistent woody stems from or near ground level, and trees, which produce a distinct trunk. A further distinction is made between those which lose their leaves when dormant and those which retain their leaves. The former are said to be deciduous and the latter are referred to as evergreens.

2

Growth

A STEM with its leaves is called a shoot and an entire stem with all its branches and leaves is often referred to as a shoot system. The chief functions are the production and support of leaves and flowers, and the conduction of materials to and from these organs. In addition foods are stored in stems.

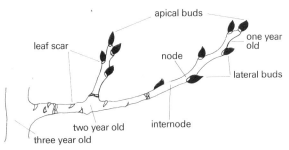

FIG 2. Shoot morphology

The point on a stem from which a leaf develops is called a node and the section of stem between nodes is called an internode. The angle between a leaf and the stem is termed a leaf axil. Buds are usually found within this axil and these are frequently called axillary or lateral buds as opposed to the terminal or apical bud, found at the tip of each stem or twig.

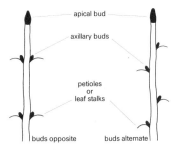

FIG 3. Bud orientation

A bud may be thought of as a compact undeveloped branch waiting for the proper stimulus to grow and develop into either another structural shoot or into a flower. There are two types of bud, naked and covered. The actual growing tip or meristematic tissue of a naked bud is protected only by the rudimentary leaves it forms. This type of bud is found mainly on herbaceous plants. Woody plants generally have covered buds which are protected by overlapping scales known as bud scales. Sometimes these buds scales are gummy or may be covered with hairs which help to protect the bud from drying out, injury and very low temperatures.

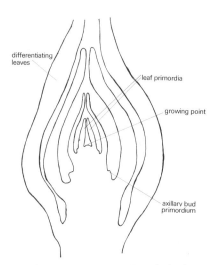

FIG 4. Longitudinal section of a bud

Not all buds grow. Those that do are referred to as active, while those that do not are called dormant. Dormant buds are usually axillary in position and situated some distance below the terminal bud. Sometimes these inactive buds develop many years after they are formed; they remain embedded in the bark as the woody stem grows in diameter and may under an appropriate stimulus grow into branches.

The increase in the length of a stem is caused largely by the rapid increase in length of the tiny internodes of the terminal bud when it develops. In most annual plants and in many woody plants of the tropics the elongation of the internodes produced by the bud continues through most of the growing season. However, in woody plants of cooler regions the elongation of these internodes occurs chiefly during a few weeks of spring.

When an axillary bud forms a twig, this develops its own terminal and axillary buds. Buds are arranged along a shoot in a characteristic pattern for each species. In some plants the buds are alternate, each successive one being on the opposite side of the shoot; in others the pattern may be spiral, or opposite. The form of a whole shoot system is determined to a large degree by the positions, arrangements and relative activities of the various types of buds. If the axillary buds are opposite, the branches produced by them are opposite; if they are alternate, the branches into which they grow are alternate. If there is a markedly dominant terminal bud with a relatively large number of dormant axillary buds, the branch on which these buds occur will be much elongated with relatively few side branches. If on the contrary the terminal bud is slow growing and the axillary buds are active, the stem grows slowly in length and will possess many relatively fast-growing branches.

It is important that anyone wishing to train a plant should develop the habit of carefully observing details of bud placement and relative activity.

It is also most important to realise that the various organs of a plant compete for the resources available within that plant. Different organs take precedence at different times of the year in response to different internal and external influences. The result is the characteristic growth cycle for that particular species. Of particular importance is the phenomenon of apical dominance.

Apical Dominance

In simple terms the terminal bud of a shoot is normally dominant. By this we mean that this bud grows more rapidly and is physiologically more active than the lateral buds which grow only slowly or remain dormant; this is referred to as apical dominance. If the terminal bud is removed, the lateral buds immediately below the cut start to develop and one or more of these soon establishes dominance over the lateral buds further down the stem.

Plant growth is controlled by the production, transport and interaction of various growth substances, sometimes referred to as plant hormones.

Different parts of plants have differing abilities to produce growth substances. Dominant buds produce a plant growth substance which has the effect, on interaction with other growth substances in the lateral buds, of inhibiting the development of those buds. While this material is being produced and transported to the lateral buds a restraint is placed on them which prevents them from developing. However, as soon as it stops the restraint is removed and they are able to develop. Therefore when a dominant bud is removed, the growth substance is no longer produced and the laterals immediately below are able to develop.

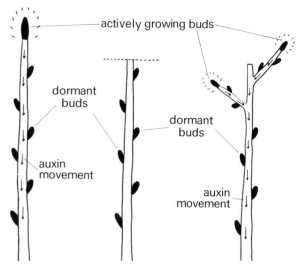

1. Dominant apical bud produces auxin which keeps lateral buds dormant

2. Apical bud removed

3. Lateral buds grow in absence of auxin and establish apical dominance over lateral buds lower down the shoot

FIG 5. Apical dominance

Once a lateral has started to develop the production of the growth substance by other developing laterals has little effect providing all the laterals are growing at a comparable rate. Several new shoots are often formed which jointly inhibit buds further down the stem.

This phenomenon has several important implications, both to normal plant shape and to plant training, although different plants react in somewhat different ways.

In general the faster the dominant bud grows, the more growth substance it produces and the greater is its dominance. If growth of this bud slows, insufficient growth substance may be produced and laterals may be able to break dormancy. It is well known that when the main branch of a young tree is forced into a horizontal position it grows more slowly and becomes less able to dominate its laterals. Use of this is made in stimulating fruit-bearing lateral shoots at the expense of vegetative terminal growth, by training branches of fruit trees to a horizontal position.

Similarly, in spring, when all the buds on a perennial plant are dormant, dominance will not be established until some time after growth of several buds has started. It is probably for this reason that so much branching of perennial plants occurs at the beginning of the growing season in temperate climates. Furthermore, when the apex stops growing in the late summer a new growth of laterals sometimes ensues ("rameaux de Saint Jean" or "Lammas shoots").

People often top trees and shrubs to make them smaller. However, they remove the dominant terminal buds in doing this and stimulate a greater number of shoots which, in time, add to the original problem rather than easing it. For this reason it is often better to thin trees and shrubs by removing whole branches at their source than to top them.

In some cases it is desirable to promote dense bushy growth. This can be achieved by the frequent removal of terminal buds. Clipped hedges are formed in this way, as are exhibition plants of Fuchsias.

Our knowledge of apical dominance can be used when deciding where to make a pruning cut. If we make a cut immediately above a bud which faces outwards, we can be reasonably sure that this bud will make a new branch which will grow from the centre of the plant and not inwards where it would cross other branches and cause overcrowding. Similarly if a tree has two adjacent shoots of equal vigour, by cutting these to two different lengths, the longer and higher one will take dominance over the other.

PLATE 6
Dormant (and some adventitious) buds growing from the stump of Moreton Bay Fig, *Ficus macrophylla.*

PLATE 7
Closer view of dormant and adventitious buds growing from the stump of *Ficus macrophylla.*

3

Stem Structure and Function

AS NOTED in Chapter 1, the shape of a plant represents the specific solution which that plant has made to the problem of presenting its leaves to the sun and at the same time withstanding environmental stresses such as wind. The stems form the framework or skeleton of any plant and as was seen in Chapter 2, besides acting in this way, stems conduct materials to and from the leaves and buds, act as storage organs and have the ability to extend themselves.

Unlike the framework of a building, stems are complex living organs which deserve considerable respect, so before we cut or modify them in any way it is important to know something of their structure and function.

Stem anatomy varies as much as does the external appearance of different plants and there are endless variations. However, a basic distinction can be made between the soft or herbaceous stems and woody stems. Some soft or herbaceous stems develop into woody stems as in the case of the young growth on trees; in other cases they do not develop further—for instance, the stems of annual plants.

The anatomy of plants is a complete study in itself and we cannot go into much detail in a book of this size. However, an examination with the naked eye of a cross or transverse section of a mature woody stem shows two major groups of tissue; the bark, which forms the outer layer of the stem, and the wood or xylem, which lies inside the bark. In some plants, right in the middle of the stem there is a small core of pith. Basically water and dissolved minerals absorbed by the roots from the soil move upwards in the xylem, while elaborated organic materials, synthesised in the leaves, move downwards in the phloem, which is a very thin layer on the innermost side of the bark.

While a plant is actively growing and is bearing leaves, a constant stream of water moves up through the stems and evaporates from the leaves. This movement is known as the transpiration stream. The quantities of water lost by transpiration are often very great and dramatic figures can be produced to illustrate this point. For instance, it has been calculated that as much as 8,200 litres (1,800 gallons) of water can pass through a single large apple tree in a six-month growing period.

If a woody stem is examined more carefully with a microscope a single layer of meristematic cells or

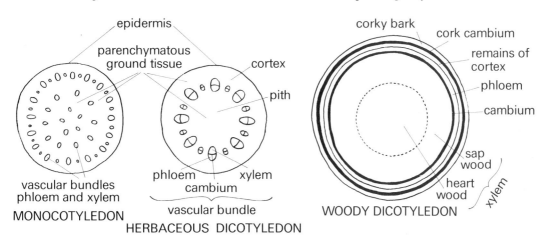

FIG 6. Transverse section through stems

cells capable of frequent division and reproduction can be found in the form of a continuous circle between the wood and bark. This layer is called the cambium. Cambial cells form new cells transversely, chiefly adding to the wood, but to a limited extent to the phloem as well. In this way the stem grows in diameter.

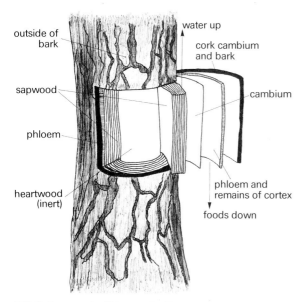

FIG 7. Movement within woody stems

Labels: outside of bark • water up • cork cambium and bark • sapwood • cambium • phloem • heartwood (inert) • phloem and remains of cortex • foods down

The bark is very thin and smooth in young stems but grows thicker and rougher with age. A secondary cork cambium is formed which adds material to the outside of the bark. If this did not happen the outside of the stem would rupture as the wood inside expanded. As a stem grows the proportion of wood to bark increases enormously so that the major part of the volume of the larger limbs and trunks of trees is wood. This is partly due to the fact that all the wood formed is retained within the stem, while the outer portion of the bark is continuously sloughed off.

In areas with well-defined growing and dormant seasons the new wood is laid down as distinct concentric rings (as seen in cross section). These are known as annual rings. On examination the rings are seen to be made up of two fairly distinct bands of xylem; an inner portion called the spring-wood in which the cells are large, and an outer portion known as the summer-wood, in which the cells are smaller. The large-celled spring-wood, which was formed with the initial flush of growth after dormancy, appears lighter than the smaller-celled summer-wood formed when growth had slowed down. Each pair of light and dark rings represents a single year's growth and from this the age of trees can be guaged by counting the rings. Foresters take core samples from trees with a special tree borer and count the rings to assess maturity.

A similar method of ageing young trees or twigs on older trees is to count the number of terminal bud scars formed along the stem. This can provide useful information when pruning.

When we come to look at the structure of herbaceous stems we can divide them into major groups; monocotyledons and dicotyledons. Monocotyledonous plants are derived from seeds containing only one seed leaf or cotyledon and are easily recognised by their thin, strap-shaped leaves with parallel veins and their flowers, whose parts are typically made up in multiples of three. Examples of monocotyledons are grasses, lilies, irises and orchids.

Dicotyledonous plants are derived from seed containing two seed leaves or cotyledons and typically have broad leaves whose veins are arranged in a netlike manner. Flower parts in this sort of plant are typically found in multiples of four and five.

Basically, herbaceous stems consist of an outer protective epidermis enclosing an area made up of unspecialised cells known as parenchyma. Through this parenchyma or ground tissue the vascular material passes as separate bundles or strands made up of both phloem and xylem. In the dicotyledons the bundles are arranged in a circle, while in monocotyledons the bundles are more evenly spaced throughout the ground tissue. The bundles of dicotyledons have cambium cells separating the phloem from the xylem, while those of the monocotyledons, which rarely form trees, do not.

In woody plants strength and rigidity are obtained by the massive central mass of wood built up in each succeeding year. In herbaceous stems which usually last for only a single growing season or subsequently develop into woody stems, the tissues are arranged to give the greatest strength for the material available. In the case of the dicotyledons this is achieved by arranging the vascular material into the form of a hollow cylinder. In the case of monocotyledons the arrangement confers flexibility and resilience rather than rigidity.

4

Ways to Train Plants

TRADITIONALLY plant training has been achieved almost exclusively by mechanical means. Even today this is the main way of training plants. Only in very specialised cases, such as the dwarfing of trees by the Japanese art of Bonsai, are cultural procedures of nutrient and water regulation employed.

However, in the last two or three decades several new ways of controlling plant growth have started to filter through to horticulturalists from basic plant research. Today we can therefore recognise five main ways of modifying plant growth. These are: (a) Mechanical, (b) Budding and grafting, (c) The use of plant tropisms, (d) Plant breeding and (e) Chemical means.

Mechanical

Mechanical means consist mainly of the removal of various parts of plants and the tying of shoots to some kind of framework. Removal of plant parts may be achieved by the removal of buds to prevent unwanted shoots developing, or by removal of shoots after they have developed. Removal of buds is generally referred to as disbudding, while removal of developed shoots is pruning.

These two operations are considered in some detail in subsequent chapters.

Budding and Grafting

Most roses, tree fruit and citrus varieties, together with an appreciable number of woody ornamental plants, are grown on the roots of closely-related plants, rather than on their own. This is done for a variety of reasons.

In some cases the variety or species used as rootstock is resistant to certain soil diseases, whereas the "scion" variety, the one which produces the fruit or flowers, would be susceptible to those same diseases if it were grown on its own roots.

Often budding, one of the ways of obtaining plants which grow on the roots of another, makes best use of available propagation material. A single twig may provide ten buds and thus ten plants, whereas that same twig might only provide one or at best two cuttings.

For some plants, particularly citrus and pip fruit, the root stock used has a profound effect upon the size and vigour of the scion variety and the quality of fruit produced.

Plant Tropisms

Plants exhibit irritability or an ability to respond to various stimuli from the environment. Stems, roots and leaf stalks (petioles) are able to respond to these stimuli and the responses are called tropisms.

With the exception of certain dramatic examples such as that of the sensitive plant *Mimosa pudica*, which quickly closes its leaflets when touched, or the Venus flytrap, *Dionaea muscipula*, which is able to shut the jaws of its modified leaves quickly enough to trap flies, plant reactions are too slow to see by simply watching. However, by observation at regular intervals or by means of time-lapse cinematography, plant tropisms and other movements can be clearly observed. The phenomena to which plants respond and the resulting tropism are as follows:

Gravity	—	Geotropism
Light	—	Phototropism
Water	—	Hydrotropism
Touch	—	Thigmatropism
Electricity	—	Electrotropism
Magnetism	—	Magnetotropism
Chemicals	—	Chemotropism.

Tropisms in which an organ moves towards the source of the stimulus are termed positive, while those which result in movement away from a stimulus are called negative. Therefore upright stems are positively phototropic, but negatively geotropic, while roots are positively geotropic. All these responses are important in determining the shape of a plant in relation to the total effect of environmental factors.

PLATE 8
Negative geotropism. These two plants of *Chenopodium amaranticolor* were both growing vertically. Three days before the photograph was taken the plant on the right was pushed over to an angle of about 45 degrees from vertical. As a response to gravity, the youngest tissues have curved so that the growing point is restored to its original orientation.

Phototropism is important in determining the arrangement of branches and leaves in relation to a plant's light source. The stems and leaf petioles bend so that the leaves are presented to the best possible advantage with regard to the light. It is for this reason that plants growing in situations where the light comes from only one direction, such as against a wall or under a tree, tend to be lop-sided, the leaves facing the source of the light. Adding to this effect is the phenomenon that shaded buds are less likely to break dormancy than those exposed to light. If carefully observed, leaves will be seen to form a mosaic arrangement so that they shade each other as little as possible.

PLATE 9
Positive geotropism. *Rosmarinus officinalis* 'Prostratus' is a mutant form of the ordinary upright Rosemary. Here the normal negative geotropism of shoots has been altered to the positive geotropism more normally associated with roots. This change totally alters the plant's shape, and gives us a valuable trailing plant.

Geotropism ensures that roots grow down into the soil and hydrotropism ensures that a plant seeks out supplies of water. Thigmatropism, the response to touch, is important to climbing plants as it enables the shoots of some species to twine around objects and thus obtain support. In other species, thigmatropic tendrils are used for climbing.

There are relatively few examples of the direct harnessing of plant tropisms by man to alter shape, but a good example is found in the forestry practice of planting trees close together to obtain long straight trunks. Here the plants mutually shade each other and the plants grow ever upward in search of light, instead of branching laterally as they would if there were adequate side light. A similar use of close planting and resulting phototropic response is found in certain flower crops where long straight stems are required.

Plant Breeding

The main aim and achievement of the plant breeder with regard to plant shape has been the production of dwarf forms of many types of plant.

Horticulturalists have demanded dwarf compact plants of many species of both ornamental and crop plants. These have a variety of advantages over taller plants, the most obvious being that they take up less room, are easier to manage when harvesting and carrying out other operations and are more wind stable. It is possible to dwarf plants by other means, but it is much more convenient if a plant grows naturally to the desired shape.

Chemical Plant Control

In Chapter 2, it was noted that plant growth is largely regulated by the movement and interaction of growth substances within a plant. One of the most exciting developments of recent years has been the identification of some of these substances and the acquisition of a better understanding of how they work. The study is, in many ways, still in its infancy and more basic research is needed. However, a few of these materials have been artificially synthesised along with a greater number of closely-related chemicals. An increasing use is being made of these to control plant growth, particularly to suit factory farming methods.

Although at present these are mainly being used by farmers and commercial horticulturalists, a few growth-controlling substances are becoming available to the home gardener. It seems likely that some of these will become standard practice in the years to come, in the same way that gardeners have come to accept the use of rooting hormones for the propagation of plants from cuttings.

Many aspects of plant development can be regulated by the use of chemicals. Early experiments looked at prevention of pre-harvest fruit drop, increased fruit set and induction of seedless tomatoes, inhibition of storage sprouting of potatoes, inhibition of tree buds to prolong dormancy, regulation of flowering, defoliation, thinning of fruit and use as weedkillers. In a very few years this list has grown to enormous proportions covering practically every important crop plant and all manner of variations of uses, although the actual number of chemicals used to achieve these results is relatively small.

Growth control substances can be divided into six major classes, namely:

Auxins, Gibberellins, Cytokinins, Abscisins, Ethylene generators and growth retardants.

AUXINS

The main uses of auxins are to promote rooting of cuttings, to control fruit thinning, increase yields of certain field crops and as weedkillers. It is of interest to note that the widely-used hormone weedkiller 2, 4-D (2, 4-dichlorophenoxyacetic acid) when applied at very low rates controls flowering and fruit thinning of certain crops. It is only when used at relatively high rates that it acts as a selective herbicide. The N-arylphthalamic acids are being used as self-topping agents in tomato culture, where they reduce the labour requirement for training. They also have the ability to induce large fruit trusses.

GIBBERELLINS

These were first discovered by Japanese scientists shortly before World War II. Their study was only taken up by Western scientists in 1955-56, since which time an enormous amount of work has been carried out with them. There are currently thirty-two known gibberellins, although only two or three are used in horticulture. There are several significant uses of gibberellic acid. It has revolutionised the production of seedless grapes for table use and has recently improved raisin production by increasing berry size. Twenty-five per cent of navel oranges are sprayed in California to increase the life of the fruit, both before and after harvest.

When used on red-tart cherries gibberellic acid stimulates shoot growth and increases flower bud formation the following year. In certain climates gibberellic acid may prove useful for the promotion of fruit setting of apples and pears where crop failures can occur through poor pollination and night frost.

Flowering can be stimulated prematurely in some vegetable crops for seed production. Gibberellic acid is used to increase the length of celery and rhubarb stalks and to break dormancy of potato tubers to obtain uniform crop emergence. It also plays an important part in the production of hybrid seed of various vegetables and is used to increase flower size of some ornamental plants such as zonal pelargoniums.

CYTOKININS

These were discovered in 1955 and have been used mainly so far to prolong the post-harvest life of green vegetables and flowers. They are showing promise, however, for use in controlling fruit set and shape of certain crops.

ABSCISINS

The structure of Abscisic acid was only determined in 1965 and it has not yet had time to be developed for horticultural or agricultural use. However, it has potential for practical application as it accelerates abscission (separation from plant) of fruits and leaves. Dormancy is induced and prolonged in the shoots of deciduous trees and tubers. The flowering response of certain plants is also altered.

ETHYLENE GENERATORS

The product Ethrel (2-chloroethylphosphonic acid, first available in 1968) when sprayed on plant parts generates ethylene, which controls plant growth in a number of ways. Some of its uses are the abscission of fruit for mechanical harvesting, the acceleration of fruit maturity and the induction of uniform ripening.

From the plant shape aspect, an interesting development has been the promotion of "bottom-break" branches of roses for cut-flower production.

GROWTH RETARDANTS

Maleic hydrazide: This was the first synthetic plant growth inhibitor to receive wide practical use. It first appeared in 1949. It prevents storage sprouting in onions, potatoes and some root crops. It is used to suppress suckering in tobacco and also to retard grass growth in areas such as motorway median strips.

Chlormequat (CCC or Cycocel–2-chloroetyltrimethyl-ammonium chloride): This is the most widely-used growth retardant in agriculture today. A major use is on wheat in appropriate regions of the world. It has the effect of producing short, stiff straw which is resistant to lodging or blowing flat.

Another important use is in the controlled growth of flower crops, particularly those sold in pots throughout the year, such as Poinsettias and chrysanthemums. Other effects such as resistance to cold, drought and salt, are induced in some plants.

Alar-85 (B-9—N, N-dimethylaminosuccinamic acid):
This is used to produce short compact plants, particularly bedding plants and especially petunias. It is estimated that 65 per cent of all bedding plants produced in the USA are treated with Alar.

Remarkable results have been obtained on tree fruits where reduced tree growth has significantly increased flowering in the following season.

Increased yields have been recorded when used on potato haulms and peanut plants. In addition Alar-85 is proving promising for enhancing the rooting of cuttings of ornamental plants such as Poinsettia, zonal pelargonium, chrysanthemum, carnation and Dahlia.

Although many of the methods outlined in this chapter may seem outside the range of the home gardener, it is important to remember just how quickly these developments have been made and adopted. Similar developments with weedkillers, insecticides and fungicides become available to home gardeners, after considerable commercial testing and usually in the safest possible form.

Similarly, it is important to think of plant training in all its aspects, particularly where unwanted growth can be prevented, and not just in terms of pruning.

1 First stage in development of a pyramid Fuchsia. Here the lowest laterals are being lightly trained along temporary canes.

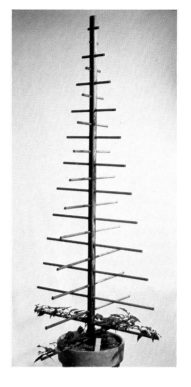

2 The same plant one month later planted in a larger pot and fastened to a permanent framework.

3 Thirteen months' growth has completed the plant's framework but the top third requires additional filling out.

4 The plant allowed to flower. This photograph was taken a further two months after 3. The plant required a further season to obtain satisfactory cover of the top framework; however, notice how uniformly flower is borne over the whole plant. The variety 'Timothy Hammett' is suitable for training into most shapes except hanging baskets.

5 An ideal whip for training into a standard Fuchsia.

6 The same whip three months later with the basis of the head well formed. Note how the leaves have been deliberately retained right down the stem.

7 A half standard formed at the same time as the plant shown in 6, flowering in the open garden after two years growth. Variety 'Baby Storm King'.

8 Young bush shaped Fuchsia in 4 inch pot.

9 Same plant as in 8 five months later, in 12 inch pot, at peak of flowering. Variety 'Flirtation Waltz'.

10 Basal shoots on a sweet pea plant to be grown on the cordon system, ready for the selection of the strongest.

11 The strongest basal shoot selected and tied to the bamboo cane.

12 The whole line of plants six weeks later. Note the uniformity of growth and the sawdust mulch.

13 A closer view of the plants showing the vigorous growth, and enlarged leaves.

14 The whole line a further six weeks later at its peak producing top quality exhibition blooms.

15 *Rosa multiflora* clone IOWA 60/5. This is one of the many strains of *R. multiflora* used as an understock. The flowers clearly show why it is often known as the Japanese blackberry rose.

16 *Rosa chinensis* 'Major'–a rose used for understock under glass or in hot climates. It is, however, a beautiful rose in its own right.

PART II

5

The One-Year Framework

ALTHOUGH it was noted earlier that annual plants are less subject to training than are woody perennial plants, there are notable exceptions to this. Tomato and cucumber plants when grown under glass are intensively trained to make best possible use of the available space. Sweet peas and culinary peas are trained on the cordon system when used as exhibition subjects. Similarly, herbaceous perennial plants such as Dahlias and chrysanthemums are treated as annual plants when they are grown to produce exhibition blooms or commercial cut-flowers.

Tomatoes

Tomatoes are, perhaps, the single crop to which most applied horticultural research has been devoted over the last twenty or thirty years. It is not therefore surprising that there are a number of ways of training them. One of the latest is simply to grow the plants large enough to produce one truss of fruit. The plant is encouraged to devote all its energies to this end, after which it is replaced by another young plant.

PLATE 10
Tomatoes are grown as single cordon plants under glass and are trained up strings hung from the roof.

Despite developments such as this, the traditional system is the one most extensively used, both under glass and in the open, by both home gardeners and commercial growers. It is essentially a cordon system, which means that a main stem is trained up a support. The flowers and fruit are produced directly from this stem, all lateral shoots being removed as soon as they start to form. In essence, as with all plants trained on a cordon system, all of the plant's energies are directed towards fruit formation, rather than vegetative growth.

Under glass it is traditional to support the plants by twisting the main stem round a string hung from overhead wires. Outside, it is usual to tie the main stem to a stake, commonly forming part of a wigwam, with other stakes up which other tomato plants are trained. Such a structure stands up well to winds.

When the plants have reached the desired height and have produced as many trusses as the grower considers desirable or possible, the main growing point is

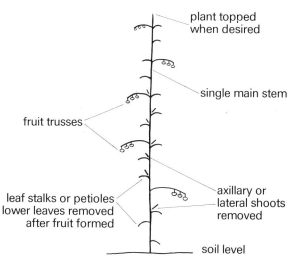

FIG 8. Tomato grown on the cordon system

29

removed or the plant topped. All the plant's remaining efforts are then directed to the formation and ripening of the remaining fruit. Outside plants are generally stopped when they have reached the top of their support stake, but under glass plants are often taken horizontally along the overhead support wires and even down strings further along the house.

When the fruit on the lowest trusses are fully formed it is a good practice to remove the lowest leaves. This is not essential, but it has the advantages of making the fruit easier to pick, it allows better air circulation, which is important in disease control, and it is more hygienic as by this stage of growth lower leaves have usually served their function and are becoming moribund.

One point worth making with regard to the training of tomatoes is that it is unwise for smokers to handle the plants. It has been clearly shown that tobacco virus diseases can easily be transmitted to tomato plants simply by handling them after smoking. These viruses can cause severe commercial losses.

Cucumbers

In warm areas cucumbers are normally grown outside and are allowed to sprawl on the ground untrained. In such areas an early crop, or catch crop after tomatoes, is often attempted under glass. Usually the plants are simply encouraged to climb up string supports by their tendrils and left pretty much to their own devices, again with little or no training.

In cooler climates and countries, particularly England, cucumbers have to be grown under glass. In such areas the culture of cucumbers has become specialised and the management of the cucumber house was for many years the yardstick by which a gardener's skill was measured.

Traditionally cucumbers have been grown in long low houses as the plants require plenty of heat and humidity and this design provides the most economic structure. Wires are stretched horizontally 23 cm (9 in) apart, about 30 cm (12 in) from the glass, and the plants are trained over these, up the sides of the house and overhead, forming a complete lining of foliage from which the fruits are suspended into the body of the house.

The main stem is grown vertically and is usually stopped at a height of about 1.2 m (4 ft) to give the side branches or laterals a chance to develop. Later one of these laterals is used to extend the plant's framework up to the apex of the house. If the laterals produce fruit at the first and second nodes, they are stopped at the second leaf beyond the second node. If not they are allowed to grow until they do produce

PLATE 11
Hothouse cucumbers are carefully trained around the inside of their glasshouse to make best use of the available light, and so that fruit may be easily picked.

fruit and are then stopped, allowing one or two leaves beyond the fruit.

The basic aim is to develop a system of leaves which can make best use of the light available, and at the same time prevent the shoots from becoming crowded. Discretion is necessary in achieving this aim and the grower will learn to remove some shoots completely and sometimes to replace them with stronger ones from nearby. Pest and disease control is made more effective when the growths are well spaced.

Sweet Peas

The sweet pea is the only true annual plant which has specialist societies devoted to its cultivation as an exhibition flower. Much of the activity of these societies centres on training the sweet pea to produce the finest blooms. Consequently a great many articles and books have been written on this one small aspect.

Basically, however, the system is the cordon system used by tomato growers. Traditionally, sweet pea fanciers grew their plants simply as culinary peas, using twiggy sticks as supports. To obtain bigger flowers on longer stems the plants were restricted to three or four main shoots. However, like many discoveries, the development of the sweet pea cordon system arose from an accident.

One year, some time before 1910, a well-known Welsh sweet pea exhibitor called Tom Jones found that some of his rows of sweet peas had been blown down by a storm. He cleared up by tying up the centre shoot of each plant and cutting away the broken and tangled lateral growths. When these plants recovered they produced better blooms with longer stems than the undamaged plants growing normally. Over the next year or so Tom Jones deliberately experimented and cut away the lateral shoots on a proportion of his plants until he was satisfied that the method worked, then he trained all his plants in this way. By 1912 the method had made its impact and was being adopted by other exhibitors. It was, however, not referred to as the cordon system until sometime during the 1920s.

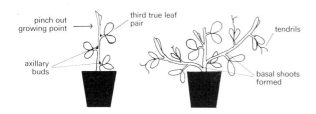

FIG 9. Stopping and formation of basal shoots in sweet pea

The system differs from the tomato system in that the true main shoot which develops from the seed is not used. Instead the main growing point is removed when the seedling has formed three pairs of leaflets. Basal shoots develop at or near ground level and the strongest of these is selected to form the main stem of the plant. It is believed by sweet pea exhibitors that the true main stem is incapable of producing a satisfactory framework. However, "stopping" has become so woven into cordon mystique that it is never seriously questioned. In addition sweet pea plants grown for exhibition are always raised in pots and only the best of these planted out. Here stopping has the advantage of keeping the plants tidy while in the pots and encourages extensive root development in relation to aerial growth.

Such a root system, when established after planting, provides a sound foundation on which to build the very vigorous stem growth which occurs during spring and early summer. The nature of the plant is altered by the system to the extent that the leaves become very large, 12-15 cm (5-6 in) wide, and the

flaps of tissue, called wings, which run down the main stem become enlarged as do the appendages (called stipules) found at the bases of the petioles. These responses to the method of training effectively increase the photosynthetic area of the plant without increasing the number of stems and leaves. These enlarged tissues contribute to enlarged flowers. The tendrils are removed at the same time as the lateral shoots to prevent them clinging to flowers and damaging them.

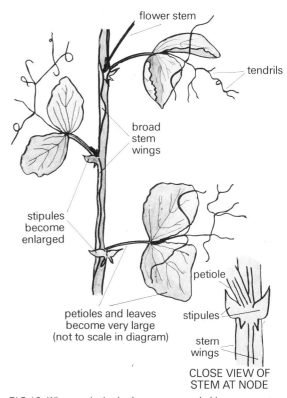

FIG 10. Wings and stipules become expanded in response to the cordon system of sweet pea training

An interesting use of plant tropisms is made in this method of growing sweet peas. In a season the plant is capable of forming 5-6 m (16-20 ft) of main stem. Normally the support canes are no more than 2.5 m (8 ft) as bamboo canes are generally difficult to obtain over this length, and the plants become hard to handle above this height and also more susceptible to wind damage. To overcome this the practice of "layering" or "dropping" has developed. Here the stems are removed from their supports and laid on the ground, which is usually covered with straw first. As the plants are normally of fairly uniform height it is possible to lay the stems along the row and then train the top 30 cm (12 in) or so of growth up a cane further along the row. This top growth is invariably soft and easily broken, therefore many growers have found it best to take the plants along as far as their new cane, but to make no attempt to refasten them for several days. After this time the tip of the plant will have turned upwards as a normal negative geotropic response, and may then be easily fastened to the cane.

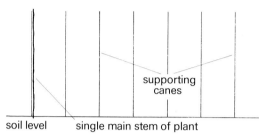

soil level   single main stem of plant

1. Plant up cane (only one plant shown)

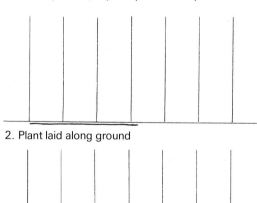

2. Plant laid along ground

3. Plant tip has curved upwards by negative geotropism and may be fastened to cane

FIG 11. Use of plant tropism in cordon training of sweet pea

Culinary peas are sometimes grown on a cordon system to produce the finest pods for exhibition. Here plants are usually raised by direct sowing and the true main shoot is used—otherwise the system is the same as for tomatoes and sweet peas, although layering is not normally practised.

Dahlias

When grown for exhibition and cut flower production, Dahlias are raised from cuttings taken from the tuber formed by the previous year's growth. This plant is treated as an annual and new plants are raised each year. By this method the grower has complete control over plant shape from the start and only young vigorous tissues are employed. Plants grown from tubers can be satisfactory for garden decoration, but in keen competition work it is felt that the old woody tissues associated with previous years' growth can reduce plant vigour to the detriment of the flower.

Dahlias exhibit a very wide range of types, both regarding plant habit and flower form and as with sweet peas many books have been written on them. Flowers range from less than 5 cm (2 in) in diameter to over 30 cm (12 in).

The training of Dahlia varieties is determined by the type of Dahlia and the use to which it is to be put. Commercial flower producers grow only the smaller-flowered types and aim to grow as many blooms as possible on acceptable stems, while the exhibitor aims to produce the best possible quality blooms within the size limits laid down by the authority controlling their exhibition.

Training begins when the plants are planted out. At this stage the growing point of each plant should be removed. This encourages lateral shoots to develop from the leaf axils once the plant has become established. If carried out at this stage it helps the plant by reducing the demands on the roots while they become established.

When the lateral shoots have reached 10-15 cm (4-6 in) the shape of the plant can be assessed and some of them may be removed to ensure a well-balanced plant. This matter of balance or symmetry is important, as Dahlias are usually supported within some form of restraining cage, either individually or as double lines. It is undesirable and impractical to support every lateral shoot formed, but if the plant is well balanced it is much less likely to be damaged by wind and makes excessive support unnecessary.

If the plant is one of the large-flowered varieties, all but three or four lateral shoots should be removed; this is known as "de-branching". With the smaller-flowered varieties only the odd weak lateral need be removed.

For the largest blooms the theory is to direct all of the plant's energies into three or four main branches, each of which terminates in a single bloom. When removing branches of such plants only one shoot should be left at each node. Shoots on alternate sides of the plant should be removed at each successive node to retain the balance and stability of each plant. This also ensures that the blooms mature at different times.

Later, when the flower buds form, a certain amount of flower bud removal or disbudding should be carried out to ensure good blooms with adequate stems for cutting. With the larger blooms, flower and

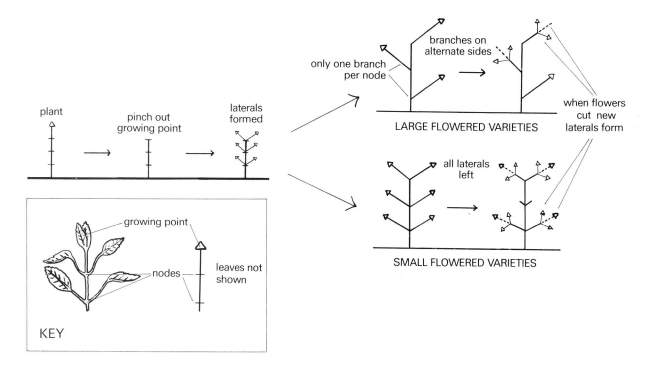

FIG 12. Dahlia training

sub-laterals will be removed for a greater distance down each shoot than with the small-flowered types.

When the blooms are cut for use, side branches lower down each branch develop and take the place of the flower just removed. This method of training is therefore a renewal system which ensures good-quality blooms throughout the season.

Chrysanthemums

In essence the method of training chrysanthemums is the same as for Dahlias. A distinction must be made between plants grown for garden decoration and those grown for cut flowers and exhibition. Also a distinction has to be made between early-flowering kinds, which flower in autumn, and late-flowering varieties, which flower during winter. The early-flowering kinds are generally grown in the open ground, while the lates are grown in pots outdoors during summer and are taken into a greenhouse during autumn to flower during the winter.

Plants of all types are raised from shoots arising from the stools produced by the previous year's growth. These are taken as cuttings. Planting is the same as for the Dahlia, except that stopping is carried out only at planting time for certain types. Spray types may be stopped at planting time to encourage the maximum number of laterals, which may in turn

be stopped several more times during the season to produce the largest possible number of flowers per plant.

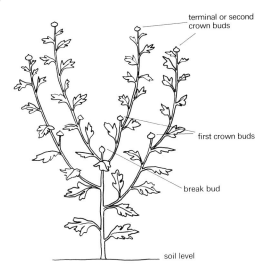

FIG 13. Chrysanthemum training

For exhibition work, with both early and late types the time at which stopping is carried out has a critical effect upon the time of flowering for each individual variety. It is important therefore to obtain

33

detailed local information for this specialised pursuit which has a strong following in a number of countries. There are a great many chrysanthemum societies, both local and national who provide detailed local information on the aspects of varieties and their timing for show work.

If unstopped the chrysanthemum behaves somewhat differently from the Dahlia. If a chrysanthemum is left to develop naturally, it will extend itself as a single stem until a flower bud is formed. This is called the "break-bud". The chrysanthemum is a short-day plant, which means that it requires short days, or more correctly long night periods, before it is able to flower. Therefore if the young plant has been planted out in the spring as would be normal, this break bud simply aborts, which has the same effect as stopping the plant by removal of the growing point. Lateral shoots are then formed, which in turn, after a period of growth, form a bud called the "first crown bud". This will flower normally in some varieties, usually early-flowering ones, or may, like the break bud, abort and give rise to further laterals. These form "second crown buds" or "terminal flower buds".

Most cut-flower and early-flowering varieties are flowered on the first crown buds, while spray and late types are often flowered on second-crown buds. As with Dahlias, large-flowered types are restricted to a few main branches, while smaller-flowered kinds are allowed to carry a dozen or more branches. Only

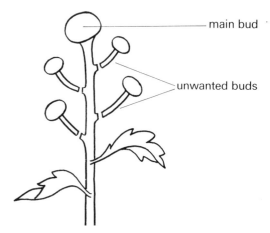

FOR LARGE FLOWERS ONLY ONE BUD SHOULD BE ALLOWED TO DEVELOP ON A SHOOT. UNWANTED BUDS SHOULD BE REMOVED OVER A PERIOD OF DAYS, NOT ALL AT ONCE

FIG 14. Chrysanthemum disbudding

one flower is allowed to develop on each branch, unless a spray of blooms is desired.

Disbudding is best carried out progressively. Distortion of the main flower bud can occur if all other buds are removed at once. Similarly, if some buds are left in reserve for a while one of these may be used should the main one become damaged.

6

Woody Perennial Plants

A. Ornamentals

Modern ideas on the use of ornamental plants in a garden design embody the concept that a plant has an intrinsic natural beauty when allowed to develop freely. Its shape is determined only by its inherent genetic make-up and the climatic restraints of the area in which it is to be grown.

This means that each plant has to be carefully chosen for every position. It is not satisfactory to plant a forest tree in a small home garden or a suburban street and expect to keep it a reasonable size by annually cutting pieces off it. It is far better to choose a small tree or a shrub in positions where considerations such as power lines become important. If a mistake is made in the choice of a plant we should not be afraid to dig it out and try something else. The old adage that a "bad plant takes up as much room as a good one", can easily be rephrased as "a

bad choice takes up as much room as a good one" Remember, if an ornamental plant is unpleasing in appearance through having to be topped or otherwise mutilated, it is a failure.

It follows that the vast majority of plants planted as garden features will need no attention other than the occasional removal of a crossed, weak or damaged branch and in some cases the removal of dead flowers.

The exception to the above is in the case of specific plants such as dogwood, *Cornus sp.*, which is grown for the winter colour of its young stems, and Buddleia, which flowers on young growth. Here it is desirable to cut the plant back hard to encourage as much young growth as possible. This should be carried out in spring for plants such as dogwood, and after flowering for plants grown for their flowers, such as Buddleia.

PLATE 12
A shrub which has been clipped so that it has lost its natural shape. Such a shrub, although well clipped, has neither natural beauty nor the design function of well-executed topiary.

PLATE 13
Few conifers have the ability to produce shoots from mature wood. This Norfolk Island pine, *Araucaria heterophylla*, has been ruined by having its main growing point removed. As it was likely to interfere with the power lines these should have been rerouted or the tree completely removed.

PLATE 14
Mutilation of pohutukawa, *Metrosideros excelsa*. Badly-torn limbs, stumps and bushy, lax untypical growth resulting from brutal cutting.

Conifers, particularly, should be cut as little as possible. Generally speaking, many of them will stand a certain amount of light tipping of lateral shoots to maintain symmetry, and indeed some species are well suited for use as hedges. However, with the exception of yew, conifers do not carry dormant buds on the woody parts of stems and branches, so that if cuts are made into the mature wood of conifers, no regeneration takes place. Similarly if conifers are topped, most of them simply degenerate for a number of years before finally dying.

A great deal of ugliness could be avoided if people would remove whole plants rather than try to compromise by mutilating unsatisfactory plants.

The modern concept of not wishing to interfere with a plant's natural shape is probably a reaction to man's over-urbanisation and domination of his environment. For centuries, however, man has been fighting the wilderness and has until very recent times been happy to demonstrate his domination of nature by training plants into various artificial shapes.

PLATE 15
Trees which should have been removed. These trees grow far too large to be planted as close as this to houses or beneath power lines. They have been mutilated to the point of being "visual-pollution"!

This desire has taken a number of forms. Plants have been clipped to form formal hedges with both practical and aesthetic functions. As an adjunct to this, plants, particularly box and yew, have been clipped into various shapes and used as living statuary. This skill is known as topiary. More recently plants such as Fuchsias have been trained into various geometric shapes as a test of a gardener's skill and for competition work.

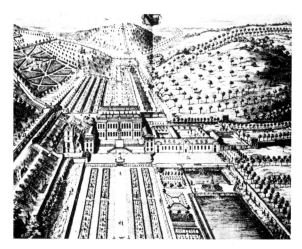

PLATE 16
Man once sought to demonstrate his dominance of the wilderness by radically altering large areas of land around his home, as shown in this eighteenth-century illustration.

FUCHSIA TRAINING

Consideration of the training of Fuchsias is a useful excercise because the principles and shapes are applicable to all other woody perennial subjects. Fruit trees, with minor differences of detail, can be trained by the same methods for special purposes, such as fans against walls and espaliers in the kitchen garden. Similarly, the principles underlying Fuchsia training are the same as in topiary, although the practical details may differ slightly.

Basic Shapes

The basic shapes into which Fuchsias are trained are bush, standard, fan, espalier, pillar and pyramid. There are additional variations but these are the basic forms.

Different varieties of Fuchsia show different habits of growth and it is important to choose a variety suitable for each shape. Generally, strong-growing varieties with fairly upright growth, although not too erect, are most suitable for the above shapes, but these would be quite unsuitable for a hanging basket, where a lax pendulous habit is required. Similarly, the very large-flowered varieties often have sparse straggly growth and are not suitable for detailed training. Some of the older, smaller-flowered varieties have the best growth habit with the added advantage that the finished shape can be covered with a very large number of flowers uniformly spaced over the plant.

Bush

This is the simplest shape and is obtained by pinching out the growing point of a young plant when it has grown about 15 cm (6 in) high. This causes laterals to develop from the leaf axils by loss of apical dominance. These are in turn pinched out, when they are long enough, leaving two pairs of leaflets. Again laterals are formed, which are in turn pinched out when long enough. This process is continued until the plant has reached the desired size and it is decided that it should be allowed to flower. Depending upon the climate and conditions under which a plant is grown, the final stop should be made six to eight weeks before flowering is desired.

To obtain a symmetrical plant uniform lighting to all sides of the plant is necessary. This can be obtained in pot-grown plants by turning each plant a half or quarter turn regularly every two or three days. Similarly, discretion must be exercised in the pinching; some laterals may grow too quickly and need to be pinched to one pair of leaves, while another may grow too slowly and may need to be stopped after it has formed three pairs of leaves.

Sometimes shoots arise from beneath the soil. these are usually vigorous and can be incorporated

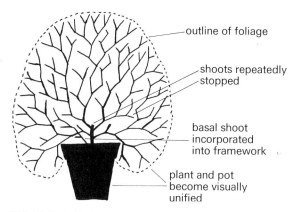

FIG 15. Bush Fuchsia

- outline of foliage
- shoots repeatedly stopped
- basal shoot incorporated into framework
- plant and pot become visually unified

into the framework with advantage. It is important to have a clear picture in mind of the shape required and then to manipulate the plant material at each stage of growth to obtain this end. No two plants behave in exactly the same way and a decision has to be made for each shoot.

Plants may be maintained for several years by pruning back to the main framework at the end of each season and then treating the new growth formed in the following spring in the same way as the laterals of the new plant grown steadily from a cutting.

Standard (or Tree)

These are in essence bushes borne on a single stem. Three main sizes of standards are recognised by Fuchsia enthusiasts, and are determined by the length of clear stem between the soil and the lowest branches. The exact definitions vary somewhat from country to country, but a commonly accepted formula is as follows:

Full standard—75-100 cm (30-40 in) clear stem.
Half standard—45-50 cm (18-20 in) clear stem.
Quarter standard (or Table standard)—no more than
30 cm (12 in) of clear stem.

Standards are trained by selecting a vigorous plant grown from a cutting. This is trained up a cane without being stopped. It is important to have the cane longer than the plant, otherwise it is easy to break the top of the plant. The long straight plant produced is usually referred to as a whip, and these may sometimes be bought for training into standards.

When the desired length of clear stem is reached, the whip should be grown on until at least another six to eight pairs of leaves have been formed, then it should be stopped. Laterals will develop at the top of the whip through loss of apical dominance, while others lower down the stem should not. The laterals

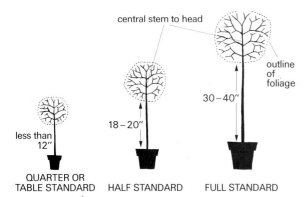

FIG 16. Standard Fuchsias

central stem to head

outline of foliage

30 – 40"

18 – 20"

less than 12"

QUARTER OR TABLE STANDARD   HALF STANDARD   FULL STANDARD

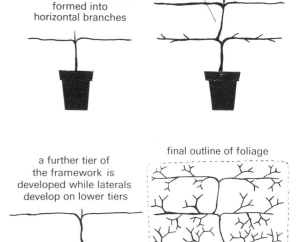

the plant is stopped and the lowest laterals are formed into horizontal branches

a sublateral is used to extend to the next level

final outline of foliage

a further tier of the framework is developed while laterals develop on lower tiers

pinching of sublaterals while framework forms ensures adequate foliage and flowers

FIG 18. Stages in the development of an espalier Fuchsia

above the desired length of clear stem should be developed into a head in exactly the same way as a bush plant by successive pinching.

As the head is developed, laterals lower down the stem and at soil level are likely to arise. These should be rubbed out as they appear.

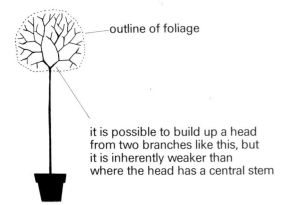

outline of foliage

it is possible to build up a head from two branches like this, but it is inherently weaker than where the head has a central stem

FIG 17. Poorly-constructed standard Fuchsia

The biggest mistake people make when trying to train standards is that they remove the leaves up the main stem too soon. These should be left until the head is fully formed and ready to flower. They contribute to the growth of the plant and if removed too soon can seriously slow down growth.

Fan, Espalier, Pillar and Pyramid

The bush and standard are the easiest shapes to form and are consequently the ones most commonly seen. The remaining shapes, the fan, the espalier, pillar and pyramid require an application of our knowledge of apical dominance. They all have to be built up from the base, as extensive laterals can not be developed if a main vertical shoot is allowed to exert dominance.

All these shapes require a framework on to which the plant can be trained. The espalier and pyramid are essentially similar except that the espalier is basically two-dimensional, while the pyramid is three-dimensional. The neatest and most satisfactory support can be made by using a square stake through which holes have been drilled, and dowelling of appropriate diameter and length inserted.

The shapes and sequence of training are illustrated in the accompanying diagrams and photographs. For the fan, espalier and pyramid, the tip of the young plant chosen is pinched out and laterals are trained on to the framework. When they have reached their desired length, they are stopped and further laterals induced to form. One of these is then chosen to extend the main framework to the next level, where it is stopped and the process repeated. Continued pinching of shoots not trained into a framework should be carried out to fill in the shape with plenty of foliage. Once the framework has been formed, which in the case of pyramids may take at least two years, pinching of sub-laterals can cease and flowers

support framework not shown
in subsequent diagrams

plant is stopped and laterals are
tied to framework – these are each
stopped when about 12″ long

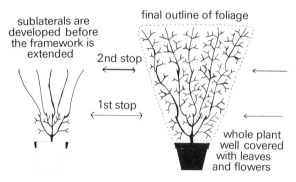

sublaterals are
developed before
the framework is
extended

final outline of foliage

2nd stop

1st stop

whole plant
well covered
with leaves
and flowers

FIG 19. Stages in the development of a fan Fuchsia

allowed to form. These should then occur over the whole plant, giving a cascade effect of bloom.

A pillar which should be of similar dimensions for the whole of its height, without any appreciable taper, may be formed like a pyramid or may be produced on a two-stem system. One is formed in the manner of a bush, while the taller one is formed like

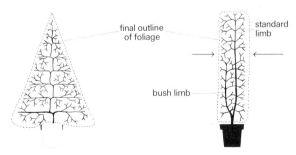

final outline
of foliage

standard
limb

bush limb

A PYRAMID FUCHSIA IS
BUILT UP IN STAGES LIKE
AN ESPALIER, EXCEPT
IT IS THREE DIMENSIONAL
AND TAPERS TO THE TOP

A PILLAR FUCHSIA IS
ESSENTIALLY A COMBI-
NATION OF A BUSH AND
STANDARD MODIFIED
TO FORM A TALL
UNTAPERED PLANT

FIG 20. Pyramid and pillar Fuchsias

a standard. The two systems meet in the middle and merge.

Endless variations of shape have been tried with Fuchsias and fruit trees over the years, but the basic phenomenon of apical dominance and the way it is harnessed determines what may be achieved. In all cases with any subject, it is important to check all ties regularly to ensure that these do not become too tight as the stems increase in diameter.

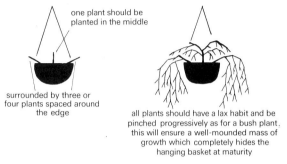

one plant should be
planted in the middle

surrounded by three or
four plants spaced around
the edge

all plants should have a lax habit and be
pinched progressively as for a bush plant,
this will ensure a well-mounded mass of
growth which completely hides the
hanging basket at maturity

FIG 21. Fuchsias in hanging baskets

TOPIARY

The art of topiary has been known since antiquity and has had its ups and downs of popularity. It was very popular between the sixteenth and eighteenth centuries. The main plants used have been box, yew and holly, although rosemary, juniper, whitethorn, privet and Mediterranean cypress have all been used.

FIG 22. Various topiary shapes

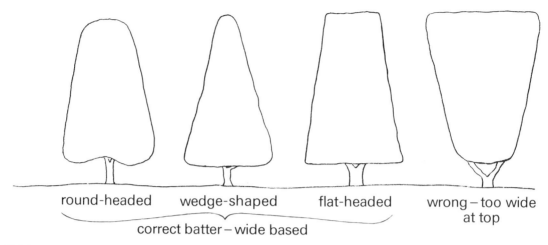

round-headed   wedge-shaped   flat-headed   wrong – too wide at top

correct batter – wide based

FIG 23. Hedge shapes

The plants chosen need to be hardy and long lived and have the ability to stand regular clipping. All manner of animal and geometrical shapes have been produced and some stately homes have had areas laid out as a game of chess and battle formations using topiary figures on lawn.

Unlike the training of Fuchsias, less attention is paid to individual shoots. A basic framework is usually established by training suitable shoots to a simple metal or wooden framework. Laterals are produced freely by the plants used and these are then shaped with shears or scissors to the desired form. As the topiary figure matures, the matrix of laterals becomes more dense as the twigs interlace.

In India, where topiary is quite popular, one method is to produce a wire-mesh framework like that used for the skeleton of a *papier mâché* figure. This is erected over the young plant or plants to be trained, As the plant grows any shoots growing through the mesh work are cut off 3 cm (1 in) or so beyond it so that in time the whole figure is filled out and the mesh hidden.

FORMAL HEDGES

A wide range of plants, both evergreen and deciduous, may be used for formal or clipped hedging. The requirements of longevity, hardiness and ability to stand clipping are similar to the requirements topiary, but they are less stringent for hedges. It is important to clip subjects such as privet and *Lonicera nitida* fairly hard and frequently when young, increasing their height in stages, rather than to allow them to grow to their ultimate height and then stopping them. By clipping from the early stages, good basal laterals will be developed and the hedge will not "open out" at its base with age.

Ideally, good hedges are wider at their base than at their top. This batter prevents shading of the lower parts of the hedge and minimises damage from wind, rain or snow.

B. *Dwarf or Bonsai Trees*

In recent years there has been a vogue in western countries for dwarf trees grown in very shallow containers. These are usually referred to as Bonsai trees, a Japanese name which means literally tray-tree and refers to the very shallow trays or pots in which the plants are grown.

The practice of dwarfing trees seems to have originated in China, but was raised to the level of a meditative art by the Japanese, particularly during the early part of last century. Unfortunately, as frequently happens when an art style is taken over by another culture and becomes fashionable it is liable to both deteriorate and to be susceptible to exploitation. There have been bad cases where tree seed has been sold for exorbitant prices as "Bonsai seed", together with a simple list of growing instructions. Similarly, although good examples of dwarf trees have been produced by westerners, more often the selection of unsuitable species and impatience have resulted in poor specimens with leaves far too large for the size of plant.

The production of a traditional Japanese specimen involves an almost religious concentration on detail as with many of the Japanese schools of flower arranging.

A good Bonsai tree should be a perfect miniature imitation of a mature tree which has been shaped by the elements. Many of the most prized specimens were in fact originally shaped in just this way in the wild. Naturally-dwarfed trees may be found in a number of localities, especially high up on mountains, on rocky ground exposed to severe climatic conditions. In such cases the skill of the grower lies in successfully transferring such plants to a shallow container and maintaining their shape, often for a hundred or more years.

Dwarf trees may be produced directly from seed or cuttings. Here the shape is determined from the outset and growth is channelled to the desired shape by all means of weights and wire devices. Each case determines the details and these depend upon the desired shape, the species and the ideas of the grower himself.

The secret with all Bonsai lies in maintaining a balance between aerial and root growth. Root growth is naturally restricted by the small container, aerial growth has to be constrained by a constant nibbling of the foliage so as to attain and maintain the shape which makes the plant desirable. Dwarf trees are living, growing organisms, not statues, and growth needs to be maintained, although reduced to as low an ebb as possible, by the correct amount of feeding and watering.

FIG 24. Bonsai tree

The soil for deciduous species is usually renewed each year, but for conifers less frequently. (Roots may be cut or tied during repotting to help restrict growth.) Similarly, organic-based liquid feeds are applied as indicated by the condition of the tree. The culture of these trees is nearer a religion than a craft or science and they require constant attention if they are not to die. The shallow container itself means that watering must be attended to perhaps as often as three to four times a day in summer.

A common mistake which many people make is to think of Bonsai trees as house plants. They should always be grown outside, preferably in a shade or lath house where they can be placed near eye level and their form fully appreciated.

The container in which any one specimen is grown is of considerable importance, not only regarding size and shape, but also concerning proportion, colour and texture. These are all things which must be felt by a sensitive observer; mass-produced containers and cultural formulae cannot produce works of art.

C. Fruit and Roses

The subjects of fruit and rose culture are very extensive, with many books devoted to all aspects of both. The commercial production of fruit is a major horticultural industry in most countries of the world and many of the techniques employed by modern producers are sophisticated and are increasingly mechanised. For this reason it is outside the scope of a book of this size to do more than indicate the general principles affecting the plants considered. These will provide basic guidance to the home gardener, who may, if he so desires, follow up specific topics in greater detail in specialist books. A list of books for further reading is provided in the appendix.

SOFT FRUIT
(Blackberries, Black Currants, Boysenberries, Gooseberries, Loganberries, Raspberries, Red Currants and White Currants.)

All the subjects under this heading are grown on their own roots and are in fact easily propagated in the open, with no special facilities.

Blackberries, Boysenberries and Loganberries
(Blackberries are often referred to as brambles in New Zealand and are subject to the Noxious Weeds Act 1950 and later amendments. Discretion is exercised in the case of horticultural varieties, but it would be best to check with the local authority before planting blackberries.)

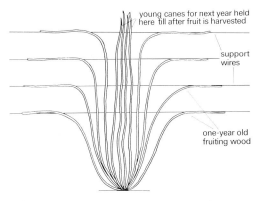

FIG 25. Blackberry, Boysenberry and Loganberry

These are all selections from, or hybrids between wild species of the genus Rubus, and their culture is very similar. The plants flower and fruit on one-year-old canes. These are trained either horizontally or as a fan on to wires stretched firmly between uprights about 1.8 m (6 ft) high. Six to eight canes per plant are sufficient. New shoots grow during the summer, while those formed in the previous season are producing fruit. The new ones should be lightly tied up, directly above the root and away from the fruiting canes. This keeps them clear of pickers and away from the older leaves, which may have become infected by various leaf-spotting fungi. Immediately after harvesting the old canes should be removed and the new ones tied in to replace them. The sooner this is done the better as it gives the young growth plenty of light and air and a chance to ripen before winter.

Raspberries

Raspberries are closely related to blackberries, Loganberries and Boysenberries and are treated in a similar manner. They fruit on one-year-old wood, but the canes do not normally reach more than 2.5 m (8 ft) in height. They are therefore usually grown vertically, restrained by a cage of horizontal wires, rather than trained along wires. After fruiting the old canes are removed to allow room for the new growths which replace them from soil level. At the end of winter it is a good idea to top the canes so that they do not exceed 1.8 m (6 ft) in height. This makes picking easier and encourages development of fruiting spurs lower down the canes.

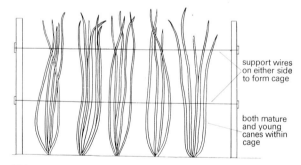

support wires
on either side
to form cage

both mature
and young
canes within
cage

FIG 26. Raspberries

Black Currants

Blackberries, Loganberries, Boysenberries and raspberries all formed a natural grouping, being species of the genus Rubus. Black currants, gooseberries and red and white currants form another natural grouping, being all species of the genus Ribes.

Black currants differ from the others in that they produce their best fruit on shoots produced in the

previous season. The aim of pruning is to encourage young growth to arise from or below ground level. Old wood is removed after fruiting and young growth is thinned to produce an open bush with well-spaced shoots.

shoots arise at or near soil level
in blackcurrants

fruit is borne predominantly
on young wood so pruning
reduces old wood to a
minimum while retaining a
well-shaped open bush

FIG 27. Blackcurrants

Red and White Currants

These produce fruiting spurs mainly on shoots several years old. For this reason pruning aims at producing a permanent framework on which fruiting spurs are borne. Red and white currants are grown on a leg or short trunk as this makes weed control much easier. The head of the plant is trained into a goblet shape by cutting back one-year-old growth by about a half each year, care being taken to make the cut above an outward-facing bud. Lateral shoots are shortened to about 5 cm (2 in). It usually takes about three to four years to produce a well-shaped plant. Main branches should be well spaced to allow light and air to reach the leaves and fruit and it is a good plan to shorten new laterals to about 15 cm (6 in) during the summer to aid towards this end. These are further shortened at winter pruning.

New shoots can be trained from near the crown of the bush to replace older growths should this

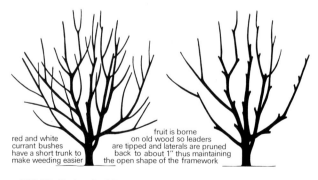

red and white
currant bushes
have a short trunk to
make weeding easier

fruit is borne
on old wood so leaders
are tipped and laterals are pruned
back to about 1" thus maintaining
the open shape of the framework

FIG 28. Red and white currants

become necessary. However, care should be taken to maintain the basic goblet shape.

Gooseberries

The gooseberry, *Ribes Grossularia*, is a plant which has had a specialist following. During the middle of last century Gooseberry Clubs were very popular, particularly in the north of England. The object was purely the sporting one of seeing who could grow the largest single berry. Not surprisingly, many forms of cultivation were tried and even today gooseberries are more likely to be grown as cordons or standards than are red or white currants, although these are equally easy to train.

• regulated pruning simply involves a light annual thinning of branches – this gives a larger crop of smaller fruit

spur pruning involves shortening one-year-old side growths to 2″ and topping some leaders – this produces a smaller crop of larger fruit

BY EITHER METHOD GOOSEBERRY BUSHES SHOULD HAVE A SHAPE LIKE THIS WITH A SHORT TRUNK WHICH MAKES WEEDING EASIER. GOOSEBERRIES HAVE SPINES

FIG 29. Gooseberries

The bush plant grown on a leg of between 15-30 cm (6-12 in) is, however, the most common shape. Early training is similar to red and white currant training, young growth being cut back by about half each year until a framework is formed. Gooseberry bushes tend, by virtue of the natural habit of the plant, to form rounded mounds rather than a goblet shape. However, branches should have plenty of space to develop without shading each other.

Once the basic framework has been established, one of two pruning methods may be employed. The simpler of these only involves the thinning out of branches to let in light and air. The other is a spur pruning method which produces fewer larger fruit suitable for dessert. Spur pruning entails hard pruning back of laterals to within 5 cm (2 in) of their bases and the shortening of all leaders by about half.

TREE FRUIT

Unlike soft or berry fruits, most tree fruit, sub-tropical fruit and roses are produced on budded or grafted plants. This was briefly mentioned in Chapter 4 and details of these operations are outlined in the appendix.

Tree fruits are sometimes called top fruit to distinguish them from soft or berry fruits which are borne on bushes rather than trees. They are grown on different root stocks, mainly to regulate their vigour in relation to environmental factors such as soil type and climate and the desired training system. Both pip fruit (apples and pears), and stone fruit (apricots, cherries, peaches, nectarines and plums) are tree fruit although all of them may be trained to shapes other than that of a tree.

Home gardeners sometimes raise trees from pips or stones, the resulting plants growing on their own roots. Plants raised in this way are referred to as seedlings as they will most likely have arisen from cross pollination and in any case will not be identical with the parent tree. Commercial varieties of fruit are clones, that is varieties maintained purely by vegetative propagation. This is carried out because they have sufficient desirable characteristics which makes them worth preserving.

When planting any grafted or budded fruit tree, the bud or graft union should be planted above ground level to prevent the scion variety from producing roots. If it did soil-borne disease resistance conferred by the understock would be lost.

Pip Fruit
Apples

The amount of information on apple culture accumulated by many years of intensive research and its practical application, in many parts of the world, makes anything which can be said in the space available here totally inadequate. Whole books have been written on pruning aspects alone and even these are superficial because of the number of training and pruning systems which have been evolved. In addition, home gardeners are more likely to inherit mismanaged trees from a succession of previous owners, each with his own ideas of pruning, than to start from scratch. This situation is further aggravated by the fact that home gardeners, unlike commercial growers, seldom specify the rootstock they require for the situation where the tree is to grow or for the training system to be followed. For this reason, only brief notes are given here, sufficient to help those who feel they would like to grow their own apples but who do not wish to go into detail, and to others who have inherited an established tree which they wish to keep.

Anyone wanting more detail should refer to some of the books listed in the appendix.

i. TRAINING A NEW TREE

Much of the research on apple understocks has been carried out in England by the John Innes Institute, which used to be at Merton, and by the East Malling Research Station in Kent. For this reason the words Merton and Malling form part of the names of the main root stocks.

Malling XII and Malling-Merton 109 produce very vigorous trees which are unsuitable for small orchards. Northern Spy produces vigorous plants and is suitable for trees to be trained as espaliers. Malling VII or Malling-Merton 106 are semi-dwarfing understocks which will produce trees suitable for the home garden. Malling IX is a stock which produces dwarf plants suitable for special shapes such as cordons.

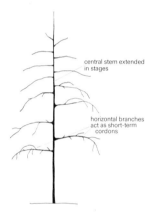

central stem extended in stages

horizontal branches act as short-term cordons

FIG 30. Spindle-shaped tree suitable for apples and pears

Modern trends in pruning and training (which are subject to fashions) lean towards small to moderate sized trees, which may be easily handled from the ground. These systems involve a minimum of pruning and worthwhile crops can be obtained early in the life of a tree. The spindle bush is a version which fulfils these aims and is easy for the beginner to manage. The shape is essentially a pyramid about 2-2.5 m (7-8 ft) high with an erect central stem from which fifteen to twenty branches are borne almost at right angles to it. The lowest of these are formed about 45 cm (18 in) from the ground and are largely developed before the central stem is extended to the next level, as in the training of a pyramid Fuchsia. These laterals are encouraged to grow horizontally by tying them down by means of strings and pegs driven into the ground. These branches do not form a long-term framework, but may be thought of as short-term cordons growing from the central stem. They are replaced over a period of years by selecting and training young shoots which

originate near their bases. The system, therefore, maintains a high proportion of young vigorous growth.

When the tree has reached the desired height, further extension is stopped. Care is taken to ensure that the fifteen or twenty cordon-like branches have sufficient space to allow good exposure to light and air and to ensure that they do not cross and rub. Short horizontal sub-laterals are left on the main laterals, but any shoots growing in a vertical direction should be cut back to 5-8 cm (2-3 in). If left they would grow up through the tree and rub against other branches.

When the main lateral branches are about four years old they should be removed and replaced. This should involve no more than three or four laterals a year. Do not forget to treat these larger cuts with wound dressing.

Overall the spindle bush system provides a small manageable tree for the home gardener with a minimum of pruning. It eliminates the formation of large old branches and keeps the plant vigorous. In addition the beginner need not worry whether he is cutting out flower buds or not, as these will form and fruit naturally on the horizontal branches. The horizontal position favours fruit formation to vegetative extension growth.

weak shape – trunk easily damaged if branch is lost

strong shape

NARROW-ANGLED CROTCHES SHOULD BE AVOIDED FOR ANY TREE EITHER ORNAMENTAL OR FRUITING

FIG 31. Crotch shape in tree

Certain varieties are more suitable for spindle bush culture than others. Generally varieties with vigorous upright growth are less suitable than varieties with a more lax habit.

ii. THE OLD-ESTABLISHED TREE

My own preference with regard to the many old apple trees of indeterminate shape and varying degrees of neglect and mismanagement found in so many home gardens, is to remove them and start again. Many such trees are often found to be extensively diseased and are simply not worth wasting time on.

However, if the tree is not seriously diseased the owner may wish to try to salvage it.

Generally, older trees in home gardens are tree- or vase-shaped with an open centre. The main stem varies in height from 0.5-2.5 m (2-8 ft) and the main branches form a framework rather like a wineglass.

The first thing to do is remove all dead, diseased and weak growths completely, then to remove all branches and twigs which cross or are too close. The aim should be to leave well-spaced, healthy laterals on the main framework so that each has plenty of room to develop and the leaves formed on them receive adequate light and air.

In the following season a lot of young vigorous shoots will be formed. These must be thinned so as to maintain adequate room for each. Those remaining can be left unpruned or lightly tipped. Fruit buds will form on these in the following season. Pruning in subsequent years should aim to keep the plant open, free of disease and vigorous so that a good proportion of older shoots may be replaced each year.

Pears

Pears are usually budded on to seedlings raised from cultivated varieties and largish vigorous trees result. Sometimes the Malling Quince A stock is used where smaller earlier-cropping trees are required. However, not all varieties of pear are compatible with quince.

Pears may be trained into any of the shapes suitable for apples and again the spindle bush is suitable for the home garden. Old trees can become very large and generally pears are less tolerant of mismanagement than apples, so there will be less opportunity for renovation.

Stone Fruit

Most types of stone fruit grown in the home garden are best trained on the small vase-shaped tree system. However, apricots and peaches are quite often grown as fans against walls especially in areas which would be marginal for free-standing trees with no protection. Similarly cherries and plums are often grown as standards.

The vase-shaped tree requires care in its establishment, but once trees have produced a well-formed framework of this shape they need relatively little pruning. This is all to the good as the less cuts made, even small ones, the less the danger of vascular diseases such as silver leaf. All that is necessary is to thin out overcrowded and congested growths after the fruit has been picked in late summer. Recent research clearly shows that there is less chance of wound infection if pruning is carried out during

summer, both because the conditions are less favourable to the disease spores at this time of the year than in winter, and because the tree is better able to counteract infection.

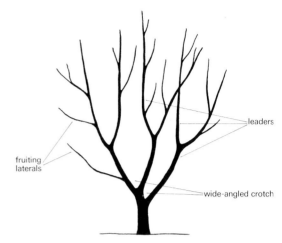

leaders

fruiting laterals

wide-angled crotch

THE VASE SHAPED TREE SHOWN HERE SLIGHTLY SIMPLIFIED IS SUITABLE FOR MOST STONE FRUIT

FIG 32. Vase-shaped tree

To establish a satisfactory vase-shaped tree it is important to lay a firm foundation while the tree is young. After planting, three strong well-placed shoots should be selected as the basis of the framework and all others cut away. The selected shoots should be pruned by as much as threequarters of their length to outside buds, which should be all at about the same height from the ground. It is important that the selected shoots should be of similar vigour.

In the following season further shoots will be formed from the three selected shoots and between six and twelve of these can be selected to form leaders; however, between six and nine would be quite sufficient. These may be selected in the growing season and unwanted growths removed. There is no point in allowing a plant to make unwanted growth and waiting until winter to remove it. Lateral growths are formed from the leaders and these form fruiting arms. Pruning should simply ensure that there are not too many of these so that overcrowding and mutual shading does not occur. An open tree also allows sprays to penetrate and give good coverage to the foliage. Once formed, pruning will only be needed to remove strong growing vertical shoots and to periodically renew fruiting arms which might otherwise become too old.

Apricots

Apricots are generally grown on plum understocks grown from cuttings, but they may also be grown on apricot and peach raised from seed.

Fruiting spurs remain productive for a number of years, but pruning should ensure that a proportion of the spurs on any tree is being renewed each year.

Peaches and Nectarines

Peaches and nectarines are treated in the same way, as the nectarine is simply a smooth-skinned peach. Both are budded on to peach seedlings, usually raised from the stones of the canning variety 'Golden Queen'.

Peaches and nectarines fruit only on lateral growths made in the previous season. For this reason pruning consists of the removal of laterals which have fruited and normal thinning of one-year-old shoots which will bear fruit next season. Care is needed to ensure that fruiting laterals are renewed over the whole length of the main leaders, otherwise there is a tendency for a tree to bear fruit high up.

Cherries

Cherries are grown on a clone of *Prunus avium* variously known as Gean, Mazzard or Malling F12/1. This is resistant to bacterial canker which can cause serious damage to cherry trees, particularly if the main stem becomes affected.

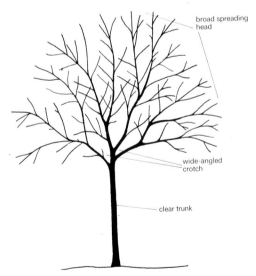

broad spreading head

wide-angled crotch

clear trunk

CHERRIES AND PLUMS ARE OFTEN GROWN AS MORE OR LESS NATURAL STANDARDS

FIG 33. Standard tree

Plants may be raised by budding in the nursery as with other fruit trees and trained in the vase shape already described, However, they are more often allowed to form a more-or-less natural standard tree with a trunk of perhaps 1.5-1.8 m (5 - 6 ft). In such cases the understock may be grown in the final position and the cherry scion budded at the height of the desired head, or the scion variety may be grafted on to the shortened branches of the understock's natural head. Plants formed in this way will provide a trunk resistant to bacterial canker and will form a standard similar to those described for Fuchsias, except that the head must be kept open, unlike the Fuchsia, so that light and air may reach all the branches.

Varieties of cherry fall into two well-defined groups, sweet or dessert cherries derived from *Prunus avium,* and sour or culinary cherries derived from *Prunus cerasus.* During the formation of the standard shape, both sorts should have their laterals shortened for about two seasons to establish a sturdy framework. Once established, sweet cherried require a minimum of pruning as they fruit on spurs formed on two-year-old and older wood. A light thinning and removal of dead twigs is sufficient. Large cuts into mature wood should be avoided wherever possible. Sour cherries, on the other hand, fruit on long lengths of thin wood produced in the previous season and pruning must ensure a good supply of these for fruiting.

Plums

Plums, like cherries, fall into two main groups, although there are further sub-types, The two main groups are European plums derived from *Prunus domestica* and Japanese plums derived from *Prunus salicina.* The European plums are hardier than the Japanese varieties which do best in warm climates. European plum varieties are budded most commonly on to Myrobalan plum root stock, while Japanese varieties are either budded on to this and other plum varieties or peach seedlings.

Besides the vase-shaped tree described for all stone fruit, plums are often trained as a standard tree with about 1.8 m (6 ft) of trunk. This is a suitable shape as the branches of many plum varieties tend to be lax and are easily weighted down when bearing a heavy crop of fruit. As with cherries, hard pruning of the main limbs forming the framework during the first few years produces a firm foundation, but once the shape has been established, plums should be cut as little as possible.

Fruit is borne on wood formed in the previous season or earlier. Light thinning of growth is advisable during midsummer, but trees should not be cut in winter as they are especially vulnerable to silver leaf infection. Similarly, plum branches need support when bearing as they are brittle and may break under the weight of fruit.

CITRUS

Oranges, mandarins, tangelos, grapefruit and certain varieties of lemon are nowadays most commonly budded on to *Poncirus trifoliata* grown from seed. This stock is semi-dwarfing, hardy and enables the scion varieties to stand lower temperatures than they would grown on their own roots. It also has the effect of bringing the trees into bearing earlier and of improving fruit quality. The lemon varieties 'Eureka', 'Villa Franca', 'Genoa' and 'Meyer' should not, however, be budded on to this understock.

Traditionally, sweet orange seedlings were used as citrus understock and may still be used where a very large tree is required.

Citrus trees generally grow naturally into well-shaped trees and require very little pruning. However, it is desirable to have a clear trunk of about 0.5-1 m (2 - 3 ft), so that lower branches do not touch the ground and so that plenty of light and air may reach the bud union and help prevent collar rot. For this reason, any shoots arising on the main stem below the main branches should be removed. Similarly, strong water shoots which grow up through the head of the tree and cross with existing branches should be removed as early as possible.

Lemons need more pruning than do other citrus, largely because they produce fruit on small twigs along much of the length of a branch, whereas other citrus varieties tend to produce fruit only on the ends of main shoots. essentially on the outside of the plant. For this reason lemons benefit from a light annual thinning of shoots and a shortening of those which are becoming too long and spindly.

SUBTROPICALS

There is a growing interest in subtropical fruits and an increasing number are being evaluated as possible crop plants. However, we will concern ourselves only with the four well-established ones, namely Feijoas, tree tomatoes, passionfruit and Chinese gooseberries. The first two subjects are tree or bush crops, while the second two are vine crops.

Feijoas (Fruit salad tree, *Feijoa sellowiana*)

Once established, Feijoas are quite hardy and can grow as high as 6 m (20 ft) although they are generally between 3-3.5 m (10-12 ft). They are allowed to grow quite naturally, with no pruning other than the removal of dead twigs. Even fruit picking is eliminated as the fruits are allowed to fall to the ground before harvesting.

Control of fruit size and quality is achieved by maintaining clones of the best types and growing these from cuttings on their own roots or grafted on to seedling roots. Hedges of seedling-raised Feijoas are quite often seen and these serve the dual-purpose of providing shelter and good-quality fruit, providing the plants were raised from good parents.

Sometimes seedling-raised plants grown in isolation will not set fruit as they require other plants for pollination. This problem does not arise when several seedlings are grown together or with completely self-fertile clonal varieties such as the American-raised 'Coolidgei'.

Tree Tomato (Tamarillo)

The tree tomato, *Cyphomandra betacea,* can only be grown in completely frost-free sheltered areas. It has large leaves, brittle stems and shallow roots, which mean that the plants must be securely staked to prevent damage.

The plants are raised in one of three ways, from seed, by cuttings, or grafting on to *Solanum auriculatum.* Grafting is carried out where wet soil and root diseases are a problem. Plants normally available at garden centres are raised from seed. These produce taller plants than cutting-raised or grafted plants. If unbranched when bought, they should be stopped at 1-1.2 m (3 = 4 ft) to encourage the development of three or four main branches.

Tree tomatoes produce fruit on the current season's growth and seedling-raised plants take several years to come into bearing. Once established, pruning consists of removing dead, diseased and crowded growth. When they have fruited, laterals should be cut back to promote new growth. The timing of the crop can be regulated by the time of pruning. Early spring pruning gives an early crop, whereas pruning in early summer gives a late crop.

Cutting and grafted plants give much lower, denser bushes, which because they were raised from plants already at the fruiting stage produce fruit earlier than seedling plants. More thinning is required on these lower plants to enable penetration of light, air and spray materials. Also, some of the lower branches may have to be removed to stop them touching the ground when they are bearing fruit.

Passion fruit *(Passiflora edulis)*

Passion fruit will withstand a few degrees of frost, but do best in frost-free sheltered sites. The plants form a vigorous vine with dense growth, which is often used to cover walls and outbuildings.

Plants are raised from seed, by cuttings and by grafting. However, seed is the main method used.

Cuttings are used for special clones and grafting is still largely experimental. Here other Passiflora species are being used as understocks in an attempt to overcome crown canker and die-back.

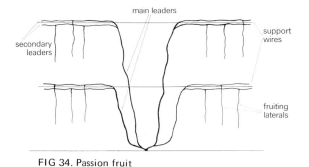

FIG 34. Passion fruit

The plants are best supported on wires, whether grown in the open or against a building. These should be at approximately 1 and 1.8 m (3 and 6ft) from the ground. This enables a clear framework to be developed and simplifies pruning. Passion fruit plants can easily form a tangled mass so it is important to establish the support and method of training right from the start and to prune the plants annually.

After planting, several vigorous shoots will develop near the base of the young plants. Four of the strongest of these should be trained along the wires as illustrated and any other shoots removed. This then forms the framework of the plant and may be established in one season of growth.

In the second year laterals will arise from the main leaders and will bear fruit. As fruit is borne on current season's growth annual pruning is necessary to provide good supplies of fruiting wood. This should be carried out only after growth has started in the spring. The later this is carried out the later the crop. Each lateral should be shortened to 15-25 cm (6-9 in.) and any weak ones should be removed altogether. After a few seasons it is advisable to renew a few of the main leaders each year to maintain a good proportion of young vigorous tissue.

Chinese gooseberries (Yang-Tao, Kiwi berry)

The Chinese gooseberry, *Actinidia chinensis,* is the only one of the four sub-tropicals considered which does not come from South America. It is indigenous to China, hence its common name. However, it has been more extensively developed in New Zealand than anywhere else and for political and commercial reasons the name Kiwi berry was thought up for export shipments of fruit during the 1960s.

The plant is a deciduous vine capable of growing to 9 m (30 ft) or more in height in its native habitat. The dormant plant is tolerant of moderate frost, but both the young growth and fruit are harmed by early and late frosts. Chinese gooseberries are maintained as clonal varieties and are normally propagated by budding or grafting on to seedling rootstocks, although cuttings may be taken. The maintenance of clones is important not only to preserve desirable fruit and growth characteristics, but because the plants are dioecious. This means that male and female flowers are borne on different plants and if raised from seed it takes at least seven years to see which plants are female and capable of bearing fruit. Male plants are necessary in a planting to provide pollen for insect pollination of the flowers and fruit set. Sometimes plants are sold with a male branch grafted on to a female plant. This enables single plants to be grown in home gardens and bear fruit. It is most important not to remove this branch when pruning, because an isolated female vine will

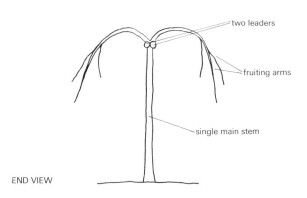

END VIEW

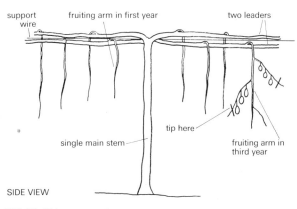

SIDE VIEW

FIG 35. Chinese gooseberry on single wire system

not produce fruit. Similarly it is important not to let the male portion, which is extremely vigorous, swamp the female part.

Chinese gooseberries may be trained in a number of ways. The simplest is to strain a single wire between two posts about 1.8 m (6 ft) from the ground. A bamboo cane is pushed into the ground and fastened to the wire by the side of a young plant. A strong shoot is selected to form a main stem, taken up to the wire supported by the cane, and other growths are removed from the young plant. When the shoot has reached the wire, it is stopped, and later, after new growths have formed at the top of this main stem, one or preferably two leaders are taken in either direction along the wire. Fruiting arms are developed at intervals along the leaders. Fruit is first formed directly on these and later on the sub laterals which arise from them. Fruiting arms are renewed every two to three years on a rotation so that each plant has a good proportion of young wood to bear fruit.

Chinese gooseberry vines are extremely vigorous and both summer and winter pruning is needed to keep to the training plan. Summer pruning is most important to keep the vines open and prevent crowding and shading. Upright growths should be removed in favour of more horizontal growths.

Laterals are thinned as they form on the fruiting arms and those remaining are shortened to seven or eight nodes beyond the last fruit, this prevents them trailing on the ground.

Fruit develops only on the first three to six buds of a current season's growth. The aim throughout is to allow direct sunlight to reach all fruiting wood.

Home gardeners can grow Chinese gooseberries on a rigid flat-topped pergola, rather like a carport, and thus make an attractive, as well as useful garden feature.

GRAPE VINES

Grape vines have long been appreciated both for their fruit and as an ornamental subject. They can be successfully grown in mild climates which do not suffer from late frosts. In cool climates such as England they are successfully grown under glass.

The history of vine growing can clearly be traced back into antiquity for at least 6,000 years. Today it is grown in many parts of the world for many uses. As much mystique is associated with grape culture as with wine, its main product. Innumerable systems of training have been devised, each with its own adherents. This makes it difficult to select just one for the home gardener who lives in an area sufficiently warm to grow grapes outdoors.

Grapes are subject to serious fungus and virus diseases and to insect attack, especially the notorious *Phylloxera vastatrix*, which caused so much devastation in French vineyards last century. For these reasons, although grapes root readily from cuttings, virus-free scion material should be grafted on to suitable rootstocks. It is important to obtain the correct rootstock for the desired variety and situation.

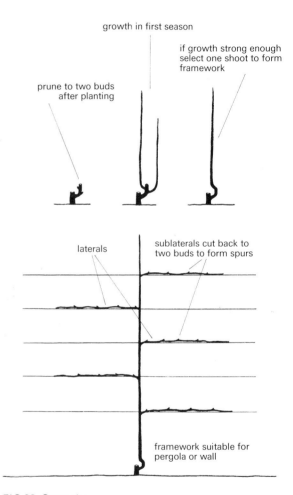

FIG 36. Grape vine

Vines are usually trained on to low fences for commercial production as this provides the cheapest form of support and makes picking, pruning and spraying simpler. However, in small areas such as the home garden, very much higher yields for the same area of ground can be obtained by training vines on to a complete overhead pergola from which the fruit may hang. In this way an extremely attractive garden feature may be obtained as well as an efficient way of producing grapes.

Irrespective of the final shape into which vines are trained, the early years concentrate on producing a firm foundation. When first planted the vine should be pruned back hard to two buds, and the roots similarly trimmed. During the first season after planting the shoots developing from the two buds should be simply supported to prevent damage and any fruit which starts to form should be removed. This enables a good root system to develop. If the growths are sufficiently strong one of them may be retained to form the foundation of the framework—if not, one of the canes should be cut back to two buds again and all others removed completely. Growth for a further season should then be strong enough for use as a framework.

If a pergola is to be covered only the strongest shoot should be retained and this should be topped at the height of the lowest wire or horizontal support. Growth in the following year will produce shoots which should initially be allowed to develop freely, before one is tied in as a lateral and another is trained up to extend the framework to a higher level. This process should be continued, probably over several years, until a main stem with suitably spaced laterals stretches from one side of the pergola and over the top.

Once the framework is established, growth in subsequent years will come from the laterals and bear fruit. After fruiting these fruit-bearing shoots should be cut back hard, leaving only two buds on each stub. These become spurs along the laterals, from which the subsequent years growth will arise and fruit. Each subsequent year the young growth from each spur should be shortened to leave just two buds.

Training under glass follows a closely similar system except that the main framework is trained up the inside of the glasshouse with the foliage close to the glass and the fruit hanging down into the body of the house, as with hothouse cucumbers.

ROSES

Roses are included with fruit as their method of propagation, namely budding on to an understock, and annual pruning has much more in common with fruit than most other ornamental subjects.

There are unquestionably more devotees of the rose throughout the world than of any other single plant. Consequently an incredible number of books dealing with roses already exists, with many new ones appearing each year. In all of these pruning is dealt with in great detail, so this section will be brief and just outline the essential details.

Commercially-raised roses are budded on to various understocks, although many varieties will perform very well on their own roots when raised from hardwood cuttings. Different understocks are used by different nurserymen in different countries. Broadly speaking, European nurserymen bud bush roses on to one of the many available strains of *Rosa canina* raised from seed. This is a very hardy species which is able to withstand European winters. It is raised from seed and to prevent suckering the bud has to be inserted into the hypocotyl, the short area of stem below the cotyledons or seed leaves but above the root. This is just below the ground in one-year-old seedling understocks and the bush produced has no appreciable leg or stem.

Nurserymen in America, Australia, New Zealand and South Africa very commonly bud both bush and standard roses on to strains of *Rosa multiflora*. This is a vigorous plant which is capable of producing large plants, but is less hardy than *Rosa canina*. It is raised from hardwood cuttings and budding is carried out about 15 cm (6 in) from the ground for bushes and 1-1.2 m (3 - 4 ft) for standards.

In tropical countries and for production of cut roses under glass *Rosa chinensis* 'Major' and *Rosa Noisettiana* 'Manetti' are employed.

Vegetatively-propagated strains of *Rosa rugosa* are commonly used for standard stems in Europe.

Different types of roses are used for various purposes and their shape will depend both on the rose itself and the purpose to which it is to be put. Broadly, several categories can be recognised for outdoor grown roses, namely Hybrid Tea, Floribunda, Rambler, Climber, Shrub Roses and Miniature Roses.

With all of these, when pruning, dead, diseased and crossed shoots are removed initially before the question of shape is considered.

Hybrid Tea Roses

Although frequently used for garden decoration, this type of rose with its high pointed centres may be thought of principally as a cut or exhibition flower. Blooms are borne on new growth, so growers aim for a well-formed open plant, with strong well-spaced shoots capable of bearing large perfect flowers.

An open cup-shaped framework of wood two or three years old is maintained at the base of bush plants, from which upright shoots are formed. Blooms are produced at the top of these, which will attain appreciable size if disbudding is carried out so as to allow only one bloom to develop on each shoot. When the bloom is removed, new branches form as with Dahlias, which will bear flowers later in the year.

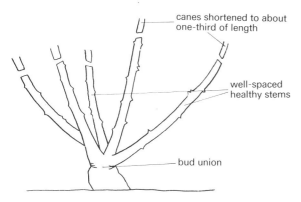

canes shortened to about one-third of length

well-spaced healthy stems

bud union

FIG 37. Open cup-shaped framework for hybrid tea rose

Young growth is encouraged to form from near the bud union so that the wood of the basic framework is kept as young, healthy and vigorous as is practicable.

Floribunda Roses

These are essentially garden plants, bred to produce masses of bloom to decorate the garden rather than for cutting to take into the home. For this reason, pruning is lighter than is general for hybrid teas, the aim being to produce as many blooms as possible and to spread these fairly uniformly over the plant. To obtain this, and at the same time maintain a vigorous healthy bush over a number of seasons, one-year-old wood is pruned lightly and bears the bulk of flowers, while older wood is pruned hard to encourage the production of young wood to form the flower-bearing one-year-old wood of the following season. This method also serves to give a long flowering season as the lightly-pruned one-year-old wood gives early flowers which is followed by later flowers formed on the new growth arising from the hard-pruned older wood.

Standard roses, whether hybrid teas or floribundas, are intended for garden decoration and pruning aims to provide a well-shaped head bearing a good proportion of flowers. Old wood should be replaced regularly, as with floribundas, but individual discretion is particularly necessary with this type of plant to maintain the shape.

Rambler Roses

True rambler roses are usually species roses or hybrids not far removed from species. They have a habit exactly similar to blackberries, Loganberries and Boysenberries and should be treated in exactly the same way. Flowering shoots should be removed after flowering and young growth which has arisen from the base should be tied back to the supports to replace the growth removed.

Climbing Roses

These should not be confused with ramblers, although both sorts are normally supported on tripods, pergolas and trellises.

Climbers are often sports or mutations, which have the characteristic of producing very strong growths, derived from bush varieties. These growths may be trained to form a framework from which young growth arises and bears flowers. Pruning of this framework should never be severe in case reversion to the original shorter form occurs. However, parts may be renewed over the years as the production of strong young growth allows. Annual pruning consists of removal of exhausted wood and the shortening back of laterals which have flowered, to four or five buds from the main framework.

Shrub Roses

This group includes a wide range of types and growth habits and includes the old-fashioned type of rose. By and large, they require a minimum of pruning other than the thinning of weak growth and a shortening of old wood from time to time, to encourage young shoots to develop from the base.

Miniature Roses

These require some attention to remove dead flowers and to maintain a compact plant bearing plenty of flowers. This is best achieved when removing spent flowers by using the opportunity to remove weak and crowded growth and to shorten strong growth. Beyond this, they require no other training.

PART III

7

Tree Surgery

PREVIOUS SECTIONS of this book have been concerned with the training and shaping of plants to a predetermined plan, from the seedling or rooted cutting stage to the mature plant. Throughout, the emphasis has been on making deliberate decisions and where possible preventing growth early on, rather than waiting until sizeable pieces of plant have to be removed.

Unfortunately people frequently inherit malformed and mutilated plants, especially trees, from previous occupants of their house and garden. Similarly, mature trees are likely to sustain injury or become attacked by a pest or a disease. Strictly it is only in such cases that surgery, "the manual treatment of injuries or disorders", needs to be employed. However, there is a growing awareness of the value of trees in our environment and builders are making more efforts to retain mature and semi-mature trees near new buildings than ever before. Often such retention necessitates the modification of the tree to fit in with its changed surroundings. Sometimes these are of a practical nature, such as making it safe in the advent of storms, stopping interference with overhead power lines and allowing adequate light to enter rooms. On other occasions they may be aesthetic considerations, such as making the tree a more pleasing shape or thinning it to allow a view to be more fully appreciated.

In a number of developed countries, tree surgery or more correctly tree care, is emerging as a recognised profession with its own skills, qualified operators and professional bodies. Although we only have space to consider the pruning of large trees, it is important to remember that tree care involves far more than simply removing branches and patching up holes. Feeding, aeration of the soil, consideration of the siting of buildings, soil levels, water table, species of tree and many other factors need to be taken into account when considering the wellbeing of plants as large as trees. Increasingly, landscape designers are consulted at

the planning stage of building projects and it is to be hoped that tree specialists will also be consulted from the earliest stages of planning.

It should be realised, from the outset of our consideration of tree surgery, that generally the pruning of large trees is beyond the scope of the layman. To start with it needs considerable skill, nerve and strength to climb into a 30 m (100 ft) high tree with the necessary tools. The weight of a single limb may be several tons, which can have devastating effects if it is not removed carefully with due consideration of lower branches, neighbouring plants, buildings and the ladders used to get into the tree. Fairly elaborate safety devices and expensive tools are now an integral part of tree surgery, which alone makes it difficult for a tree owner to carry out his own work.

Unfortunately tree work has long been a field open to abuse by unscrupulous operators. It is not difficult to convince many home owners that a tree is likely to fall on their houses unless it is lopped. Usually the tree is then ruthlessly mutilated by such people in the shortest possible time and an excessive charge made. For this reason it is very important that any owner of sizable trees should be aware of the principles involved. In this way he may ensure a satisfactory job by supervising an ordinary unqualified tree cutter or contractor. (An essential point when employing anyone on tree work is to ensure that he has adequate insurance against injury. Tree work is dangerous and any claims made for injury could be substantial. Ideally, a contract should be drawn up between owner and operator.) It is important that reputable tree-care firms organise themselves into professional bodies, with a code of ethics and a minimum standard of work. A number of countries have a national minimum set of standards for tree work.

What then are the surgical aspects of tree care?

Damaged and Diseased Parts
As with any plant of any size, damaged or diseased limbs should be removed and burned as soon as

possible. Damage may be caused by dramatic events, such as lightning, or simply by two branches crossing and rubbing against each other. Where fungus or insect attack is involved the limb should be cut back to healthy tissue, wherever this is practicable.

PLATE 17
Dead branches such as this should be removed from any tree as the first stage in pruning.

When discussing the stem structure of woody plants in Chapter 3, it was noted that whereas the outer layers of bark are continuously sloughed off, all the xylem or wood formed is retained within the body of the tree. As new annual rings of cells are added to the outside of the wood by the cambium, older rings near the centre of the plant cease to function. The conducting tubes become plugged by special cells called tyloses. In addition various chemicals such as pigments, resins and tannins become abundant in this older wood. The non-functioning older wood is referred to as heartwood, while the younger functional rings, situated outside the heartwood, are called the sapwood. The pigments and other materials in the heartwood darken it and protect it to some extent from wood rotting fungi and other organisms. For this reason, heartwood timber is more durable than sapwood timber. The relative proportions between heartwood and sapwood vary considerably between different species of tree. In some the sapwood is very narrow, only one or two rings thick, in others the sapwood can be 90-100 rings wide. Similarly in some species all the wood appears uniform with no visible difference between heartwood and sapwood, although the functional distinction is the same, only the outer rings being functional.

It is very convenient and useful to think of a woody perennial as a fairly thin living organism, growing over the remains of previous years' growth. The heartwood only acts as a support and strengthener, which can to a large extent be dispensed with. This is evidenced by venerable trees, where much of the heartwood has been either rotted or burned out, yet the tree still thrives.

Similarly, it is common to see cases where the active outer layers of a tree have grown over fencing wire and other objects attached to it.

PLATE 18
The outer tissues of trees have the ability to envelop objects close to them as they expand laterally. Here fencing wire has become embedded in the stem of a large tree.

This phenomenon of young active tissues annually increasing in diameter and enveloping objects in the way leads to knot formation in wood. These are the basal portions of branches and small twigs, which have become buried in the wood of the main truck over a period of years. This activity is frequently confused with healing, probably because the slow overgrowth of wounds by the outer layers of a tree resembles the healing of human cuts. However, the strict definition of healing embodies the concept of "restoring to health" and in the case of trees this slow overgrowth could be little further from the truth.

When a branch several years old is removed, both heartwood and sapwood are exposed. The heartwood, being non-functional, remains inert and in fact presents a good site for the establishment of infection, despite the materials contained in it, as these soon become leached out of the tissues nearest the exposed cut. Sapwood reacts to injury first by blocking off exposed cells by deposition of suberin and by accumulating gummy materials in the conducting

PLATE 19 *(left)*
Slow overgrowth of large wounds. The living outer tissues are slowly covering the wound left by the removal of a large limb. However this has already taken several seasons and will take many years to cover over completely. The wound is larger than was necessary, was not cleanly made and was untreated, making it an ideal site for fungal infection.

PLATE 20
This wound has been made correctly. The surface is clean as left by the chain saw and requires no further trimming or smoothing. It is close to the main trunk of the tree, but exposes no more wood than is necessary.

tubes, which reduces water loss. This is followed by the formation of callus cells derived mainly from cambial tissue, although a wide variety of other tissues are able to contribute. Callus cells are essentially unspecialised, but they have the ability to differentiate into cambium and cork cambium layers, which continue the growth of the outer living tissues of the plant over the wound. This overgrowth invariably takes many years, during which time the heartwood may become extensively rotted, and a cavity formed. For this reason, all wounds into all but the smallest branches should be protected as soon as possible.

Recent research has shown that modern household water-based plastic paints, intended for outside use, contain fungicides in their formulation and may be used as effective wound dressings. The advantage of these is that a colour similar to that of the colour of the trunk may be used and the wounds thus made less conspicuous. Proprietary wound dressings of the "Santar" range are also effective, but some of these have been made in bright colours for plantation work, which makes them less desirable for amenity trees. It has been found that bitumen paints are often ineffective and that turpentine paints can be harmful to a tree.

Limb Removal

The way in which branches are removed is very important, especially since the advent and ready availability of power saws. Although these are of tremendous value to professionals, they can cause trouble when used by amateurs.

First, they make the work too easy, so that branches which might have been spared through the physical effort involved by the use of hand saws, are now quickly removed. Careful assessment before making any cut is an essential aspect of tree work and the speed of power saws can lead to hasty decisions.

Second, while it is desirable to make a clean cut close to the main stem, it is possible with power saws to go too close and make an unnecessarily extensive wound.

As has already been mentioned, large branches are very heavy which means that no attempt should ever be made to remove these with one cut. Traditionally, most garden books show diagrams of under-cutting and sawing down from the top to meet the under cut. This is recommended to prevent the weight of the falling branch tearing an extensive strip off the main trunk of the tree. In practice it is very difficult to leave a clean surface when using this method. It is far better to remove the branch in segments, leaving a stub of 45-60 cm (18 - 24 in), which can then be safely removed with one final cut from the top. A branch removed in segments is likley to cause less damage than one cut off whole, which would need to be cut up after removal anyhow.

Stubs should not, however, be left on a tree as these invariably die and provide an enhanced platform for the establishment of fungal disease. Their removal should be as close to the parent branch or main stem as possible, but in such a way as to expose the smallest surface possible.

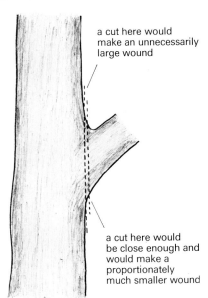

a cut here would make an unnecessarily large wound

a cut here would be close enough and would make a proportionately much smaller wound

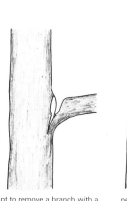

never attempt to remove a branch with a single cut – the weight of the branch will tear the trunk

never leave a stub

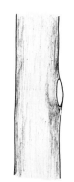

make a clean cut close to the main stem or branch

FIG 38. Tree limb removal (1)

FIG 39. Tree limb removal (2)

PLATE 21
Stubs such as this should never be left on a tree.

PLATE 22
Large limbs are best removed by removing in sections until a short stub is left. This may then be cleanly removed by a single saw cut from the top. Note the tear in the stub from the last large section of branch. Had an attempt been made to remove the branch in one go, a large tear would have been made down the trunk of the tree.

When removing limbs, remember that balance is most important, both from aesthetic and engineering considerations. If a branch has to be removed from one side of a tree it is often necessary to remove one or more corresponding branches from the head to maintain a balanced plant.

It is vitally important to view a tree from as many viewpoints as possible before removing any healthy limb. Time should be taken, as the golden rule is: *It is easy to remove a branch, but impossible to replace.*

Cavity Treatment

Cavities often form in large branches or main trunks as a result of faulty pruning. Fungi grow into the tree from untreated cuts and stubs and rot out the heartwood leaving a hollow or cavity. Sometimes this significantly weakens the branch or trunk, sometimes it does not. It depends upon the species of tree and the position and shape of the cavity. In either case, it is desirable to halt the fungus as much as possible and to encourage a larger proportion of living tissue to develop.

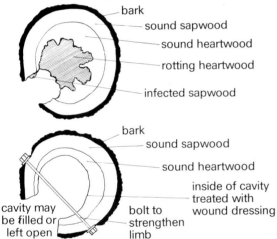

FIG 40. Cavity treatment in trees

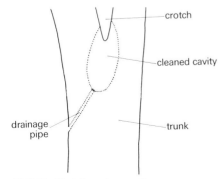

FIG 41. Draining a tree cavity

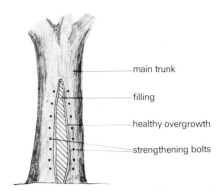

FIG 42. A well-filled tree cavity

It is important to remove as much dead and rotting wood as possible. This may be a lengthy operation and should not be underestimated. A mallet and chisel are the traditional tools for this, although power-operated gouges are available. Wherever possible a backing of sound heartwood should be left, otherwise there is a danger of the sapwood drying out and the tree dying. When the dead material has been removed, the inside of the cavity should be coated with a fungicidal paint.

PLATE 23
All wounds should be treated with a dressing as soon as possible.

57

A decision as to the structural soundess of the tree has to be made by the operator on the site, where he can take into account all the available factors. Often, if the cavity is not too extensive, he may decide that the cavity is best left open after treatment with the fungicidal paint.

Occasionally a small basal filling or drainage pipe is inserted to prevent water accumulating at the bottom of the cavity. Similarly, it may be decided that a bracing bolt is a desirable safeguard. It is important to remember that each case must be treated on its merits at the time. This requires both experience and intelligence.

Sometimes, either for structural reasons, or because it is considered desirable that the tree should grow over the cavity and cover up the hole, the cavity is filled.

All manner of materials have been used for filling cavities in trees. These include wood, brick, clay, mortar, lime, cement, cork, rubber, asphalt and plastics such as polystyrene. Ideally, the material used should have a certain amount of "give" in it, or else it will crack when the tree flexes under wind stress or simply act as a rigid core which will rub the tree from inside. The method of insertion is important to ensure that the filling knits with the tree and is not pushed out as the tree grows. When skilfully carried out the tree will grow over the filled cavity and in time it will become hardly visible.

Cavity treatments are unlikely to cure a tree of an established fungal infection, but they can make a tree safe and prolong its useful life as an amenity.

Bracing and Cabling

Each species of tree has its own intrinsic habit and branch formation. In addition, the conditions experienced early in the life of a tree affect its ultimate shape. Some trees end up with a narrow V-shaped crotch or with side branches coming away from their parent branch at an acute angle. This is an inherently weak shape structurally and the branches are much more likely to split under stress than in a tree where the branches form unions nearer to right angles with each other and at the crotch.

When a V-shaped branch does split, extensive damage invariably results. For this reason, when an arborist anticipates trouble, he may advocate bracing the crotch by the use of one or more threaded rods placed through the branches forming the crotch. Holes slightly larger than the rod are bored through the limbs and a small area of bark is removed down to the wood, large enough to accommodate a washer. The branches are pulled closer together with appropriate roping and a small winch, the bolt passed through the holes and the washers and bolts fastened. The ropes may then be released, which ensures a moderate tension on the rod; this, however, should not be excessive.

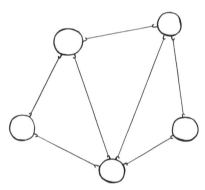

A TRIANGULAR PATTERN OF CABLING HIGH UP IN THE TREE IS THE BEST STRUCTURALLY

FIG 44. Triangular cabling of tree

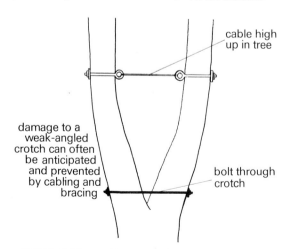

cable high up in tree

damage to a weak-angled crotch can often be anticipated and prevented by cabling and bracing

bolt through crotch

FIG 43. Cabling and bracing

Support such as this will suffice for small trees, but in large trees it is desirable to supplement this with metal cables or perhaps light chains, higher in the tree. These should be fastened by means of screw hooks inserted into the branches, or in cases of high stress a bolt-type fastening should be inserted through the limb and fastened with a washer and nut. Iron collars have been used, but these are to be avoided as they have the effect of both rubbing the tree as it moves and strangling the branch as it increases naturally in diameter. The precise stressing between branches can only be decided for each case, taking into account species of tree, wind direction and arrangement of branches. However, a system of triangulation is usually the most satisfactory from an engineering point of view.

Aesthetic Considerations

Having considered all the truly legitimate reasons for removing substantial parts of trees, we must now consider the less tangible aspects of convenience and perhaps aesthetics.

The vast majority of trees are cut today for reasons such as deprivation of light from houses, interference with power lines, views being obscured and neighbours who are concerned with leaf fall from deciduous trees. If we are to bow to these pressures, we must ensure that the tree suffers as little as possible, both physically and in appearance. Only too often the view or the power lines take precedence.

WAYS TO PRUNE TREES

There are three main ways of dealing with a tree—pollarding, heading back and thinning.

Pollarding

This is the most severe form of treating a tree and consists of cutting off all the branches of a tree at the crotch, back to the main stem. This was the traditional way of obtaining firewood from British forests

PLATE 24
This is "pollarding".

and of treating willows which were required for the production of shoots for basket making. Many trees will not tolerate such treatment and there can be no justification for dealing with an amenity tree in this way. Pollarding produces an ugly stump and any tree which has been treated in this way should be removed and replaced with a plant of suitable proportions.

Heading, Dropcrotching, Lopping, Topping and Dehorning

These terms mean slightly different things to different people. Strictly, lopping means to remove a branch off the side of a tree, but in general usage all the above terms mean more or less the same thing.

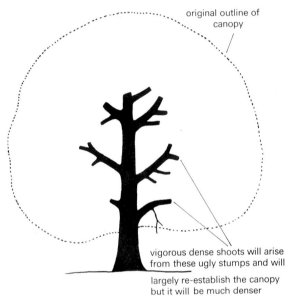

original outline of canopy

vigorous dense shoots will arise from these ugly stumps and will

largely re-establish the canopy but it will be much denser

FIG 45. A headed tree

This is the shortening of all the main branches to a greater or lesser degree. Again the method is to be deplored as it destroys the natural outline and balance of a tree, reducing all species to a common mop- or round-headed shape. However, on occasion it may be preferable to the complete removal of the tree. It is usually carried out to increase light or to expose a view. It certainly does this for a short titme but a large number of dormant lateral buds will be stimulated into vigorous growth and encouraged by the unrestricted available light, so that after one or two seasons a much denser tree results than originally. The frustration caused by this often results in a more brutal pollarding being carried out.

Dropcrotching exposes large areas of heartwood which may act as infection sites and scorching of the bark of some trees may be caused by sudden exposure to the full force of the sun.

59

PLATE 25
This oak tree was healthy and required no pruning other than the removal of a few dead minor branches. However, when in leaf, the canopy cast too dense a shade for any plants to be grown underneath, even bulbs.

A light thinning of branches and removal of some of the lowest ones was all that was required to achieve the desired effect. The shape of the tree has hardly been altered, the hallmark of good tree work.

If carried out, branches should be removed with a sloping cut, starting just above a vigorous bud or shoot, and running back and across the limb at an angle of about 45 degrees. The bud or shoot must always be at the peak of this cut and should point in the direction where new limb development is desired. Wounds must be scrupulously treated with wound dressing.

Thinning and Lifting
Thinning and lifting are the methods most to be encouraged in tree work and when skilfully carried out fulfil the idea of "a well-pruned tree appearing as an unpruned tree".
The operations are just as simple as their names. Thinning involves the removal of selected limbs, both large and small, right back to their origins. Lifting

involves the lifting of the canopy by removing the lower limbs from the main trunk. It is surprising how much light entering a house is lateral and thinning and lifting can often have a dramatic effect in increasing such light. Similarly, many views are enhanced by the framing provided by light foliage. Lifting can effectively double the height of a trunk and may raise the crown above the level of the lower windows of a house.

Other advantages from this method are that by removing branches to their origin, far less dormant buds are stimulated, and those that are, are discouraged by the shading of the existing canopy. The possibility of sun scorch to delicate bark is also eliminated. Thinning of brittle trees, such as horse chestnut or elm, lessens weight and wind resistance and often prevents branch shedding.

Thinning, as with other desirable things, does require both a greater practical skill in climbing the tree with appropriate safety equipment and an aesthetic appreciation comparable to that of a sculptor, neither of which are required for pollarding. However, this only emphasises the need for skilled operators comparable to those found in other areas of modern life, together with appropriate recognition and rewards for their abilities.

Time of year to prune and knowledge of species

The time of year to prune and an adequate knowledge of tree species cannot be set out in a book of this size. However, the old idea that trees are best pruned when dormant has been largely superceded. Gumming of the water-conducting vessels and callus formation occur much more rapidly in an actively-growing tree than a dormant one. Trees which bleed freely, such as walnut, sycamore, maple and birch should only be pruned when in leaf as the water demand of foliage on other branches helps to stem this flow. In addition the spores of many wood-rotting fungi are favoured by periods of wet weather and are consequently found in the air in lower numbers in periods of hot dry weather.

Besides these considerations there are the practical points that tree surgeons will require to work through-out the year, not just in the dormant season and that cold hands and slippery trees in winter seriously add to the dangers of tree work.

removal of lower branches effectively raises the canopy, lengthens the stem and allows much more lateral light

FIG 46. "Lifting"

PLATE 26
Another view of the thinned tree shows how it has been used to enhance the approach to the house.

APPENDIX I

Budding and Grafting

BUDDING AND GRAFTING are the means by which one woody perennial plant may be joined to another. They are most often used to join the aerial parts of one plant with the roots of another.

Budding, as the name implies, uses a single bud, while grafting uses a short length of young shoot.

Budding is carried out in summer, when the initial burst of growth made by woody perennials has had a chance to mature a little.

Grafting is best carried out in spring, when the sap is flowing freely and dormancy is just ending.

The plant supplying the roots is known as the stock, while the plant placed on to these roots is know known as the scion.

In all forms of budding and grafting the principle is to unite the cambial layers of both parts so that union and growth may quickly take place.

Budding

Young plants raised from seed or cuttings are used as stock plants, while scion material is selected from young healthy growths, also made in the current season. Care is taken to ensure that there are no stock buds beneath the bud union, which might otherwise form suckers.

In this series of illustrations the main stages involved in budding a hybrid tea rose scion on to a *Rosa multiflora* understock are shown.

Grafting

There are many ways of grafting, each with a special purpose. However, the one most commonly used for propagating woody perennials is the whip and tongue method illustrated.

Here the cambial layers of the stock and scion are brought into close contact over a wide area made possible by the slanting cuts.

The tongue of the scion helps to hold the two parts together. As with budding the wound is tightly bound and water excluded until union has taken place.

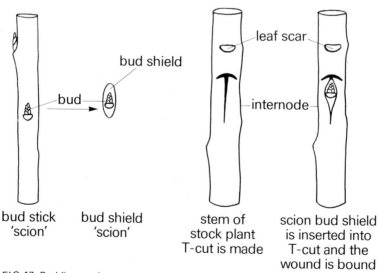

FIG 47. Budding—main steps

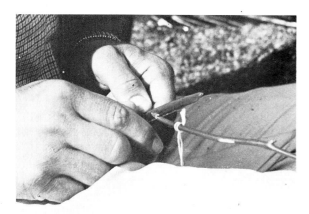

PLATE 27
The bud is removed from the budstick by a single knife cut. A piece of xylem covers much of the cambium on the shield of tissue behind the bud. This is removed with the knife.

PLATE 28
A T-cut is made in the stem of the stock. A knife pressed against the stock cuts down to the xylem and enables the bark to be lifted as two flaps. The bud is then quickly inserted to prevent drying of tissues. The somewhat disrupted cambial surfaces of both stock and scion are thus brought together and may regenerate and join.

PLATE 29
The bud is tightly bound into position with a rubber budding strip. This holds scion and stock together and prevents drying out. Rubber budding strips have the advantage over other types of binding—they perish within a month or so and do not need removing to prevent the stem becoming strangled as it grows.

PLATE 30
During the following winter the head of the stock plant is removed, leaving only the scion bud to grow.

63

PLATE 31
The top of the stock plant is painted with wound dressing.

PLATE 32
In spring the scion bud grows.

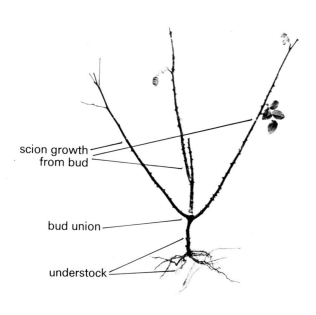

scion growth
from bud

bud union

understock

PLATE 33
A head is formed during the growing season on the stock roots. The plant is ready for sale at this stage and may be planted into its permanent position.

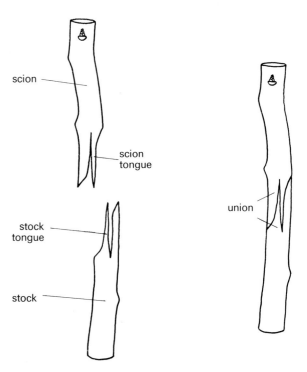

scion

scion
tongue

stock
tongue

stock

union

FIG 48. Whip and tongue grafting.

APPENDIX II

Tools and Pruning Cuts

IT SHOULD BE unnecessary to say that all tools should be kept clean, sharp and in the best possible working order. Unfortunately, many people badly neglect gardening tools and even the best of these soon deteriorate without care.

Cutting tools should be cleaned immediately after use and wiped with an oily rag; many plants have sap which will stain and corrode tools.

Knives can be sharpened on a stone at home, but saws and secateurs are best sharpened by an expert.

It is important to both the tool and the plant that the correct tool is used for each job. Secateurs are used on twigs no more than 19 mm (¾ in) in diameter. Long-handled loppers, which have extra leverage, can be used on branches up to 25-30 mm (1-1¼ in) in diameter. Above this a saw is necessary. Secateurs and loppers should never be rocked from

side to side when used on stems too large for them. Such treatment will strain the secateurs and will damage the plant. In both the blade and anvil and parrot's bill models, the cutting blade should always cut downwards.

Where few trees are involved, a carpenter's panel saw with about seven teeth per 25 mm (1 in) is adequate, but where greater use is anticipated, one of the curved pruning saws is very useful. These are able to get into awkward corners where the larger panel saw could not. In addition they cut only on the draw stroke, which makes them fast to use.

Many hedge shears have a notch in them to cut larger pieces than the soft tip growth for which the rest of the blade is intended. These should never be used for pruning, but reserved for hedge and grass clipping.

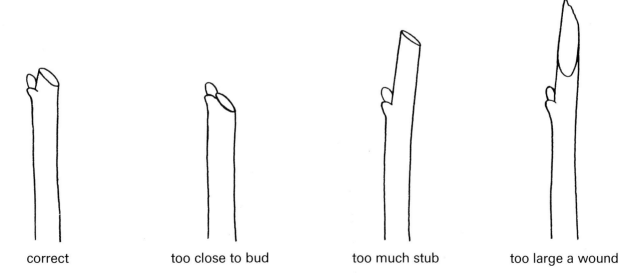

correct   too close to bud   too much stub   too large a wound

FIG 49. Correct and incorrect pruning cuts.

APPENDIX III

Book List for Further Reading

This is in no way comprehensive, but is simply a guide to books for further reading which have been found to be of value.

Sweet Peas

Janes, E.R., 1953. *Sweet Peas, a Complete Guide to Their Culture.* Ward Lock and Co., London and Melbourne.

Dahlias

Barnes, A.T., 3rd Edition, 1966. *The Dahlia Growers Treasury.* Collingridge, London.

Rooke, J.E., 1966. *Dahlias for Small Gardens.* Pan Piper Small Garden Series, London.

Topiary

Hadfield, Miles, 1971. *Topiary and Ornamental Hedges.* Adam and Charles Black, London.

Bonsai

Yoshimura, Yuji and Halford, Giovanna M., *The Japanese Art of Miniature Trees and Landscapes.* Tuttle, Vermont & Tokyo.

General Fruit

The Home Orchard. New Zealand Department of Agriculture. Wellington, 1966.

The Reader's Digest Complete Library of the Garden. London, 1965.

Apples

Thompson, C.R., 1966. *Pruning Apple Trees.* Faber & Faber, London.

Passion Fruit

Fletcher, W.A., 1970. Passionfruit growing. Bulletin 135, New Zealand Department of Agriculture, Wellington.

Chinese Gooseberries

Fletcher, W.A., 1971. Growing Chinese Gooseberries. Bulletin 349, New Zealand Department of Agriculture, Wellington.

Grape Vines

Berrysmith, F., 1970. Viticulture. Bulletin 354, New Zealand Department of Agriculture, Wellington.

Roses

Gault, Millar, S. and Patrick M. Synge, 1971. *The Dictionary of Roses in Colour.* Ebury Press and Michael Joseph, in collaboration with the R.H.S. and R.N.R.S.

Tree Care

Pirone, P.P., 1959. *Tree Maintenance.* Oxford University Press, New York.

Budding and Grafting

Garner, R.J. 1967. *The Grafter's Handbook.* Faber & Faber, London.

INDEX

Abscisins 23
Active buds 16
Adventitious buds 18
Aerial parts 14
Aesthetic considerations 59
Age of trees 20
Alar-85 24
Annual rings 20, 53
Annuals 14
Apical bud 16
Apical dominance 17, 18, 37, 38, 39
Apples 43
Apricots 45
Araucaria heterophylla 35
Auxins 23
Axillary bud 16

Balance 13, 41, 57
Bark 19, 20
Batter 40
Biennials 14
Blackberries 41
Blackcurrants 42
Bonsai 40, 41
Boysenberries 41
Bracing and cabling 58
Break-bud 33, 34
Budding and grafting 21, 62
Bud orientation 16, 17
Buds 16
Bud scales 16
Bud scars 20
Bud union 43
Bush 37

Callus cells 55
Callus formation 61
Cambium 20, 53, 63
Cavity treatment 57
Chemical plant control 22
Chenopodium amaranticolor 22

Cherries 46
Chinese gooseberries 48
Chlormequat 23
Chrysanthemums 33
Citrus 47
Climbing roses 51
Clones 43
Conifers 36
Cordon 43, 44
Cordon system 29, 30, 31
Cork cambium 20
Cotyledon 20
Covered bud 16
Crotch shape 44, 58
Cucumbers 30
Culinary peas 32
Cytokinins 23

Dahlias 32
De-branching 32
Deciduous 15
Dehorning 59
Dicotyledons 20
Disbudding 21, 32, 34
Dormant buds 16, 18
Dropcrotching 59
Dropping 31

East Malling Research Station 44
Ecological factor 10
Environment 9, 13, 19, 21, 52
Environmental factor 11
Epidermis 20
Espalier 38
Ethrel 23
Ethylene generators 23
Evergreen 15

Fan 38, 39
Feijoas 47
Ficus macrophylla 18

First crown bud 33, 34
Floribunda rose 51
Food chains 10
Fuchsias 25, 26, 37
Fungal infection 53, 57, 58

Geotropic 21
Geotropism 22, 32
Gibberellins 23
Grazing 10, 11
Gooseberries 43
Gooseberry clubs 43
Graft union 43
Grapefruit 47
Grapevines 49
Ground tissue 20
Growth retardants 23
Growth substances 17, 22

Heading 59
Heartwood 53
Hedges 40
Herbaceous perennial 14
Herbaceous plant 16
Herbaceous stems 19, 20
Hybrid tea rose 50
Hydrotropism 21, 22
Hypocotyl 50

Internode 16, 17

John Innes Institute 44

Lammas shoots 18
Lateral bud 16, 17, 59
Layering 31
Leaf axil 16
Leaf stalks 21
Lemon 47
Leptospermum scoparium 2
Life cycle 14
Lifting 60, 61

Limb removal 55
Loganberries 41
Lopping 59

Maleic hydrazide 23
Malling 44
Mandarins 47
Manuka 2
Meristematic cells 19
Meristematic tissue 16
Merton 44
Metrosideros excelsa 36
Miniature roses 51
Monocotyledons 20
Moreton Bay Fig 18

Naked bud 16
Nectarines 46
Node 16
Norfolk Island Pine 35
Noxious weeds act 41

Oranges 47
Ornamentals 35
Oxygen 10

Parenchyma 20
Passionfruit 47
Peaches 46
Pears 45
Perennial 14, 18
Petioles 21, 22
Phloem 19, 20
Photosynthesis 14
Phototropic 21, 22
Phytoplankton 10
Pillar 38, 39
Pinus radiata 11
Pip fruit 43
Pith 19
Plant breeding 22

Plant hormones 17
Plant tropisms 21, 31
Plums 46
Pohutukawa 36
Pollarding 59
Power saws 55
Pruning 21
Pyramid 38, 39

Rambler rose 51
Rameaux de Saint-Jean 18
Raspberries 42
Red currants 42
Rooting hormones 22, 23
Roots 13
Root stock(s) 21, 43, 44, 62, 64
Rose chinensis 'Major' 28
Rosa multiflora 28
Roses 50
Rosmarinus officinalis 22

Sapwood 53
Scion 21, 62, 64
Scion variety 43
Second crown bud 33, 34
Seed-leaf 20
Seedlings 43
Shoot 16
Short-day plant 34
Shrub roses 51
Shrubs 15
Silver leaf 45
Soft fruit 41
Soil 13
Spindle bush 44
Spring wood 20
Standard 37, 38, 43
Stem anatomy 19
Stipules 31
Stone fruit 45

Stopping 31, 33
Subtropicals 47
Summer wood 20
Sweet peas 27, 28, 30

Tamarillo 47
Tangelos 47
Terminal bud 16, 17
Terminal flower bud 33, 34
Thigmatropism 21, 22
Thinning 60, 61
Tomatoes 29
Tools 65
Top fruit 43
Topiary 36, 39
Topping 59
Transpiration stream 19
Tree Fruit 43
Trees 15, 37
Tree surgery 52
Tree tomato 47
2, 4-D 23
Tyloses 53

Understock 43, 44, 62, 64

Vascular bundles 20
Visual pollution 36

White currants 42
Wind-pruning 2
Wings 31
Wood 19, 20
Woody perennial 14
Woody plant 16
Woody stems 19
Wound dressing 55, 60, 64
Wound healing 54

Xylem 19, 20, 53, 63